# Shortening the Leap

From Honest Doubt to Enduring Faith

by

Robert G. Tuttle, Jr.

*First Fruits Press*
*Wilmore, Kentucky*
*c2015*

Shortening the leap: from honest doubt to enduring faith.
By Robert G. Tuttle, Jr.

First Fruits Press, ©2016
Previously published by Bristal House, 2007.

ISBN: 9781621714682 (print), 9781621714699 (digital)

Digital version at http://place.asburyseminary.edu/firstfruitsheritagematerial/120/

First Fruits Press is a digital imprint of the Asbury Theological Seminary, B.L. Fisher Library. Asbury Theological Seminary is the legal owner of the material previously published by the Pentecostal Publishing Co. and reserves the right to release new editions of this material as well as new material produced by Asbury Theological Seminary. Its publications are available for noncommercial and educational uses, such as research, teaching and private study. First Fruits Press has licensed the digital version of this work under the Creative Commons Attribution Noncommercial 3.0 United States License. To view a copy of this license, visit http://creativecommons.org/licenses/by-nc/3.0/us/.

For all other uses, contact:

First Fruits Press
B.L. Fisher Library
Asbury Theological Seminary
204 N. Lexington Ave.
Wilmore, KY 40390
http://place.asburyseminary.edu/firstfruits

---

Tuttle, Robert G., 1941-
    Shortening the leap : from honest doubt to enduring faith / by Robert G. Tuttle, Jr.
    207 pages : illustrations ; 21 cm.
    Wilmore, Kentucky : First Fruits Press, ©2016.
Reprint. Previously published: Anderson, Indiana : Bristol House, 2007.
ISBN - 13: 9781621714682 (pbk.)
    1. Theology, Doctrinal--Popular works. 2. Christian life--Methodist authors. 3. Apologetics. I. Title.
BT77.T87 2016                                                                                        230

---

Cover design by Jon Ramsay

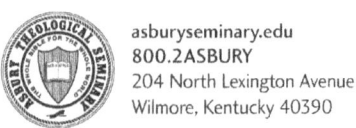
asburyseminary.edu
800.2ASBURY
204 North Lexington Avenue
Wilmore, Kentucky 40390

First Fruits Press
*The Academic Open Press of Asbury Theological Seminary*
204 N. Lexington Ave., Wilmore, KY 40390
859-858-2236
first.fruits@asburyseminary.edu
asbury.to/firstfruits

# Shortening the Leap

## From Honest Doubt to Enduring Faith

by

Robert G. Tuttle, Jr.

# Table of Contents

**DEDICATION**

**ACKNOWLEDGEMENTS**

**INTRODUCTION**  9
*"How Can I Preach What I No Longer Believe?"*
*(The Crisis)*

**CHAPTER ONE**  14
*"Why Jesus?"*
*(Exploring the Basic Content of Faith)*

**CHAPTER TWO**  25
*"Can God Forgive a Sinner Like Me?"*
*(The Importance of Repentance and Faith)*

**CHAPTER THREE**  35
*"How Can I Forgive?"*
*(Confronting the Past)*

**CHAPTER FOUR**  45
*"How Can I Overcome?"*
*(The Universal Question)*

**CHAPTER FIVE**  56
*"What about the Other Religions of the World?"*
*(Have You Read the Qur'an Lately?)*

**CHAPTER SIX**  79
*"How Can Bad Things Happen to Good People?"*
*(The Age-old Question)*

**CHAPTER SEVEN    89**
*"What about Life after Death?"*
*(How Can I Stop Grieving?)*

**CHAPTER EIGHT    100**
*"Must I Belong to a Church to Be a Christian?"*
*(Why Do I Need God, or Others?)*

**CHAPTER NINE    116**
*"What about Faith and Doubt and the Issues of Politics?"*
*(Is Jesus a Republican or a Democrat?)*

**CHAPTER TEN    129**
*"How Can I Know the Will of God?"*
*(The Future)*

**CHAPTER ELEVEN    140**
*"What About the Unforgivable Sin?"*
*(Can God's Call on My Life Be Renewed?)*

**CHAPTER TWELVE    150**
*"Is Faith in Jesus Christ the Only Way to Heaven?"*
*(The Perennial Question)*

**CHAPTER THIRTEEN    161**
*"What about the Next Generation?"*
*(Overcoming Barriers to Spirit-Assisted Ministry)*

**CONCLUSION    174**
*(The Challenge)*

**APPENDIX    178**
*(A Synopsis of the Other Major Religions of the World)*

**BIBLIOGRAPHY    205**

To

Dianne,

Honest doubt has led us both
to enduring faith.

## Acknowledgments

My wife and I have a crew of stonemasons for friends. They have helped to build the house where we hope we will spend the rest of our lives. They are men of integrity and strength. One is Ferlin Ray Brummitt, but we call him "Junior." I have tested some of this material on Junior over the weeks and months (in fact, some of this was written with him in mind). To Junior and all the gang, Lonnie Thomas (the actual head of the crew and whose quiet strength is matched only by the stones that he lays so carefully), Donald Thomas, and Marty Brummitt, a special thanks.

Thanks also to my sister Betty Newman (who is a saint) and to Sarah Campbell, Molly Warren, Jon DeMarco, John Breon, Kent Reynolds and George Callendine, all ministers and friends whom I love and admire.

As always, thanks to Debi Andrews, who is patient and kind in helping to turn mere pages into publishable form.

I must also mention my friends at Bristol Books. Their service to the Church has been faithful and true. Thank you sincerely for encouraging me over the years.

> Robert Tuttle, Jr.
> Sugar Hollow Orchard
> Fairview, North Carolina
> December 2006

There lives more faith in honest doubt, believe me,
than in half the creeds.

**ALFRED LORD TENNYSON**

## INTRODUCTION

# "HOW CAN I PREACH WHAT I NO LONGER BELIEVE?"
## (THE CRISIS)

I was standing outside my office in a theological seminary when a student walked by, obviously upset. I try never to say, "How are you?" without meaning it (though I sometimes do), so when he simply grumbled inaudibly I invited him inside. As I closed the door he began to weep quietly and then erupted into sobs. When I made an awkward attempt to console him he blurted out, "Just an hour ago I received word that I've been appointed to serve a church in my home conference, and I am now realizing that I do not believe any of it anymore. In two months time I will be the pastor of a church and I have nothing to offer—absolutely nothing! Nothing of Christianity makes sense to me anymore—whatsoever! How can I preach what I no longer believe?"

I said, "Let's talk."

He described the crisis as best he could. Then after ten or fifteen minutes of denying everything in the faith that he had once held precious, I simply said, "Frank, we need to go back to the basics. We need to talk about Jesus. Get him right and all the rest falls into place."

He flashed, "You're not listening. I don't even believe the man existed."

Somewhat surprised, I flashed back, "Whoa, there's more hard evidence for the existence of Jesus than for Julius Caesar."

Frank managed to look up, "OK, I grant you, there was a man named Jesus who walked the face of the earth 2000 years ago."

I said, "That's a start. Tell me about him."

"Well, he was a good man. He might even have been a prophet, if there is such a thing."

"OK, Frank, that's progress. In less than a minute we have gone from zero to a man named Jesus who walked the face of the earth 2000 years ago, who was a good man, a prophet, if there is such a thing. If there is such a thing as a prophet, would he have been a true prophet or a false prophet?"

Frank looked up at the ceiling; he looked back down the wall; he finally looked at me, "Do you want the truth?"

"Yes, Frank, I've got to have the truth."

Exhaling, he said, "I cannot in good conscience say he was a false prophet."

I'm thinking, "This is too easy," so I said once again, "We're making real progress now. We have a man named Jesus who walked the face of the earth 2000 years ago, who was a good man, a prophet if there is such a thing, a true prophet, so why did they crucify him?"

Frank shrugged, "Everybody knows that. They crucified him because he claimed to be the Son of God."

I added, "Then it seems to me that he either was the Son of God or he was a madman. Was he a madman?"

Once again Frank looked up at the ceiling; he looked back down the wall; he looked at me, "Do you want the truth?"

"Yes, Frank, I've got to have the truth."

"I cannot in good conscience say he was a madman. Just too much of what he had to say had the ring of truth."

I concluded, "Listen up, Dear Brother. In less than five minutes we've gone from zero to a man named Jesus who walked the face of the earth 2000 years ago, who was a good man, a prophet if there is such a thing, a true prophet, who claimed to be the Son of God, who was not a madman. You know what I would do if I were you? I think I would risk believing that he was and is who he said he was and is."

With that Frank looked at me (actually smiling) and said something I will never forget as long as I live, "You've just shortened my leap."

**A Stated Purpose**

For some time now I've been collecting questions that pose problems for people struggling with doubt. I've asked a host of different people—including students, day laborers, teachers, lawyers, stonemasons, doctors and stay-at-home moms—what challenges faith the most? Although there are a number of good books attempting to answer the age-old "hard questions," most of those tumble out of the theological or philosophical mindsets of the various authors. I wanted to address the more contemporary issues from the point of view of those actually asking the questions.

So, generally speaking, this book attempts to answer real questions about life, and (as the title, *Shortening the Leap*, suggests), provide insights for people for whom faith is a giant leap. In fact, these people tend to define faith (since it apparently lies beyond the senses, perhaps even the realm of their experiences altogether) as trying to believe in something they can't quite believe in, that's just out of reach, just beyond belief. They sometimes ask, "Must I check my brain at the door of the church or does the Christian faith make sense? Furthermore, what's the point? What's in it for me?"

This is not just a book on apologetics, however. It is a book that links the gospel of Jesus Christ to the issues at stake when speaking or doing that Good News in normal everyday encounters. I've been doing and teaching Christian theory and praxis for more than forty years. It is painfully apparent to me that what communicated just a few years ago might not communicate so well today. Oh, the message is the same, but the understanding is sometimes different. Thankfully, the old man is still learning new and wonderful things. So, there is a need for a book that addresses the issues of faith from a little different perspective, a book that seeks to move people—both within and without the Church—from honest doubt to *enduring faith*. How do we gain it? How do we find it again if we've lost it? Then, how do we help others find it as well?

I rarely encounter real atheists. Most so-called atheists are simply tossing out some notion of God that I tossed out nearly fifty years ago. Most of the world has a measure of faith in something. One of the significant things about New Age, for example, is that at least there is room at the table for a kind of spirituality. Post-modernity has a growing perception that there is more to reality than sight and reason. The challenge is not so much with atheists, or even agnostics, but (to borrow a word from my colleague George Hunter) with *ignostics*. Len Sweet refers to those distracted by cyberspace and the myriad of games available on the Internet as a culture of *vidiots*. So, my task here is to move people from doubt to faith, but also from faith to faith—from small measures of faith that perhaps just miss the mark to the kind of faith that is in touch with a reality that can move them from point A to point B, that can make a difference in their lives, that really does move mountains.

I believe that the Holy Spirit is always afoot. The first words out of the mouth of God following the Fall, "Where are you?" mean that God alone takes the initiative in the drama of rescue.

Ultimately God has more invested in our lives than we do. My prayer, even as I write these words, is that God will enable you to find something in these pages to move you from doubt to faith (or from faith to faith) so that life can be more manageable, more meaningful, and more joyful.

I do not for a moment pretend to be objective. That is the price of passion. I have an incredible bias—he is Jesus. If you expect me to give Jesus and his distracters equal time as if I were offering you a choice that is merely up to public opinion, you will be greatly disappointed. If, however, you expect me to make a case for faith in Jesus Christ that can change your life forever, then you might well be in for the greatest experience of your life

I know that faith is not always easy. For some this adventure will be more difficult than for others. Know one thing for certain: I've written this book for one reason and one reason alone—to influence you for God. Endure the bumps, but enjoy the ride.

## Chapter One

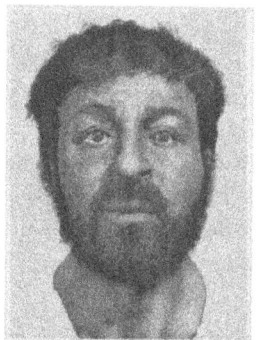

## "Why Jesus?"
### (Exploring the Basic Content of Faith)

The portrait at the head of this chapter appeared in a *Popular Mechanics* magazine a few years ago as a representation of what Jesus, as a Galilean Jew in the First Century, might have looked like. It is not particularly prepossessing. So, honest doubt wants to know why such a man still commands global attention over 2000 years after his death.

Recently a student came into class asking the question many of the youth in her church were asking, "Why Jesus?"

I love that question. What better platform for a winsome (and hopefully intelligent) presentation of the gospel. Evangelists tell us that salvation is the free gift of God. There is nothing that we can do to earn it. Then they tell us that we must repent of our sins and put our faith and trust in Jesus Christ if we are to have a relationship with God and experience the power of the Holy Spirit "to go and sin no more." So, what is the theology at work in all of this? Where does Jesus come into the picture? Why his sacrifice on the Cross? What, if anything, can faith in Jesus do that faith in the other religions of the world cannot do?

Andre Crouch says, "If Jesus is a crutch, give me two." Some of us Christians become so obsessed with communicating to a post-Enlightenment, post-Modern, post-Christendom kind of a world that we sometimes forget the simplicity of Jesus.[1] When Karl Barth (arguably the greatest theologian of the last century) was asked, "What is the most profound theological insight for Christians today?" he replied, "Jesus loves me this I know, for the Bible tells me so."

I'm a historian. My best insights are usually in retrospect. Søren Kierkegaard was fond of saying, "We live our lives forward, but we understand them backward. How can we know where to go if we don't know where we've been?" The challenges and opportunities present in the world today have never been greater. Thankfully, the enduring message of God's love toward humankind was recorded throughout the Bible and epitomized by Jesus in his birth, his early years, his baptism, his temptation, his ministry, death, resurrection and ultimately, his glorification.

The Sermon on the Mount and his Great Commission speak both the content and the call of Jesus. As a result the book of Acts captures the mindset and community impact of that content and call. The early Church really believed that Jesus said and did all of those things recorded in the gospels and that it was important for others to believe those things if they were to be put right with God and experience the power of God's Holy Spirit. So, how does it work? Again, why Jesus?

First of all, let me set the broader stage. Let me attempt to explain redemption from a cosmic perspective. Planet earth is out of orbit with God. There is a gravitational pull away from the things of God. The books of the Bible describe the cycle all too well): ". . . the whole world is under the control of the evil one" (I John 5:19).[2] Luke 4 describes Jesus (after his baptism) being driven by the Spirit into the wilderness to be tempted by the devil. At one point "the devil led him up to a high place and showed him in an instant all the kingdoms of the world. And he said to him, 'I will give you all their authority and splendor, for it has been given to me, and I can give it to anyone I want to'" (vv. 5-6). Whenever I read that passage my first reaction is always, "that's a lie." But have you ever known Jesus not to get in the face of a lie, especially a lie of such proportion? The implication is that although humankind was given dominion over planet earth (Gen. 1:26; Ps. 8:6), that dominion now belongs to Satan. God did not give it to him. We gave it to him, for a promise, or a lie, what I sometimes refer to as the biggest lie of all. Watch it happen.

> Now the serpent was more crafty than any of the wild animals the Lord God said to the woman, "Did God really say, 'You must not eat from any tree in the garden'?"
> The woman said to the serpent, "We may eat fruit from the trees in the garden, but God did say, 'You must not eat fruit from the tree that is in the middle of the garden, and you must not touch it, or you will die.'"
> "You will not surely die," the serpent said to the woman. "For God knows that when you eat of it your eyes will be opened, and you will be like God, knowing good and evil" (Gen. 3:1-4).

They did *not* become like God. Instead, they instantly became aware of their own nakedness and were ashamed. Suddenly, God's good creation became mortal and prone to sin.

Most think that the admonition not to eat of the tree of the knowledge of good and evil is about temptation. It's not about temptation. It's about choice. *If you cannot say no, your yes is meaningless.* We chose to sin and in so doing, gave the title deed to planet earth to the enemy of God. So, how and when do we get it back?

I once heard Mark Nyswander preach a sermon on Jesus as our kinsman redeemer. His logic went something like this.

In biblical times property was forever linked to the original owner. If an Israelite sold a piece of property, the title deed was sealed and registered in a public place. The original owner had the right to redeem that property in perpetuity if three things were in place.[3] First, you needed proof that you were the original owner (or a direct descendant of the original owner as kinsman redeemer). Second, you needed enough collateral for the full market value for that piece of property, and third, you needed the power and authority to remove a reluctant seller or usurper.

Now turn to Revelation 5:

> Then I saw in the right hand of him who sat on the throne a scroll with writing on both sides and sealed with seven seals. And I saw a mighty angel proclaiming in a loud voice, "Who is worthy to break the seals and open the scroll?" But no one in heaven or on earth or under the earth could open the scroll or even look inside it (vv. 1-3).

Although opinions differ as to the identification of this scroll, let's, for a moment, imagine that it represents the title deed for planet earth.[4] All of its contents are sealed and registered, but there is no direct descendant worthy to redeem the full market value or powerful enough to remove the usurper. There is weeping and despair. But WAIT! Suddenly the Lamb ("looking as if it had been slain," but with "seven horns and seven eyes") appears standing in the center of the throne of

God. As the Lamb takes "the scroll from the right hand of him who sat on the throne" all heaven breaks loose, singing, "You are worthy to take the scroll and to open its seals, because you were slain, and with your blood you purchased men for God . . . ." (vv. 6, 9). Surely, the Lamb is worthy. Let's follow the logic.

*First* of all the Lamb can prove that he is a direct descendant of the original owner because as the Incarnate Son of the living God he now has a navel.

I was once asked to debate a well-known television evangelist on the university campus of the seminary where I was then teaching. At one point my opponent gave me a bit of a nudge, "Tuttle, don't give me a Jesus in a hair shirt and a sheep under his arm, he now rules at the right hand of *glory!*" My reply, "As long as you don't give me a Jesus in a pin-striped suit and a *Wall Street Journal* under his arm, because the Jesus of glory still bears the marks of the Incarnation, and not just in his hands, his side and his feet, but in his navel, because the suffering began in the manger, not on the Cross."

All of the Incarnation was a passion narrative—cradle to grave. Mel Gibson's movie *The Passion* doesn't know the half of it. It hurts God to be squeezed into sperm and implanted in a mama.

> For this reason he had to be made like his brothers in every way, in order that he might become a merciful and faithful high priest in service to God, and that he might make atonement for the sins of the people. Because he himself suffered when he was tempted, he is able to help those who are being tempted (Heb. 2:17-18).

It has always been significant to me that God does not have to imagine how I hurt when I hurt inside; God knows how I hurt when I hurt inside because God has been here.

*Second*, the Lamb, the Son of the living God, was not only a direct descendant, he had sufficient collateral for full market value in that he was "a lamb without blemish or defect" (I Peter 1:19). As a result, when Jesus, our kinsman redeemer,

> ... had offered for all time one sacrifice for sins, he sat down at the right hand of God. Since that time he waits for his enemies to be made his footstool because by one sacrifice he has made perfect forever those who are being made holy (Heb. 10:12-14).

*Third*, the Lamb had authority to remove or defeat the entrenched enemy, Satan. Recall that the Lamb had seven horns and seven eyes—the symbol for ultimate authority throughout the book of Revelation (Rev. 5:6-14).

Surely the Lamb is worthy. Michael Card's song "Jubilee" proclaims "Jesus as our Jubilee." Ultimately, he alone fulfills the nature of the covenant first established, or cut with Abraham, but fulfilled on the Cross. He alone is our kinsman redeemer, not only of planet earth, but for our own personal salvation as well. Sacrifice in biblical times was corporate as well as individual (Heb. 9:7). Revelation speaks of the eventual redemption of the world, but the Gospels speak of the redemption of the Church, *here and now*. We have been redeemed. We need not wait until all time has been fulfilled to receive it.

Furthermore, Mark 13:10 states that this gospel must be preached in every nation BEFORE Christ will return and establish God's ultimate reign in both heaven and earth. 2 Peter 3:11-13 admonishes:

> Since everything will be destroyed in this way, what kind of people ought you to be? You ought to live holy and godly lives as you look forward to the day of God and speed its coming. That day

will bring about the destruction of the heavens by fire, and the elements will melt in the heat. But in keeping with his promise we are looking forward to a new heaven and a new earth, the home of righteousness.

Note, Peter tells the Church to *speed its coming*. My former student and friend, John Breon, comments on this thought, "Wow! Does this mean that God is depending on us to bring about conditions for Jesus' return? I'm sure that God's sovereignty is not totally dependent on our action or response. But it is amazing how far God will go, how humble God will be to include us. Second Peter 3:9 also indicates that God delays the end to give more people time to repent."

This last comment is significant as well. *Our task as the Church is not to create more programs simply to attract more people; it is to extend the ministry of Jesus.* In his farewell discourse Jesus tells us,

> I tell you the truth, anyone who has faith in me will do what I have been doing. He will do even greater things than these, because I am going to the Father. And I will do whatever you ask in my name, so that the Son may bring glory to the Father. You may ask me for anything in my name, and I will do it (John 14:12-14).

So, why Jesus? Because God created us for fellowship and wants to be known as a God of love, mercy, justice, faithfulness and longsuffering. I frequently refer to the biblical images of the gospel as *good news/bad news/good news*. The first good news is that we were created in the image of God—original righteousness—we were immortal (Gen. 1:27). It was easier to obey God than to disobey God. We were righteousness prone.

Then the bad news—original sin—so that now we are

mortal (Gen. 3:19). It is easier to disobey God than to obey God. We are sin-prone.

Then the ultimate good news that God is in Jesus Christ reconciling the world. "God made him who had no sin to be sin for us, so that in him we might become the righteousness of God" (2 Cor. 5:21).[5]

**The Parable of the Wedding Banquet**

You do not have to die to go to hell. Too many of my friends are languishing there already. The Parable of the Wedding Banquet speaks to the point. In order to understand the story fully it is important to realize that in biblical times the host (especially a king) might make preparations for a wedding banquet for months. Not only was the food and wine provided, but also the guests were given special clothes to wear. Those first invited refused to come and were punished. The king's servants were then instructed to go into the streets and gather all they could find, both good and bad. When the king went to greet his guests he noticed a man who was not wearing the garment provided. The king asked, "Friend, how did you get in here without wedding clothes?" When the man had no excuse, the king instructed his attendants, "Tie him hand and foot, and throw him outside, into the darkness, where there will be weeping and gnashing of teeth. For many are invited, but few are chosen" (Matt. 22:13-14).

The broader context provides the best interpretation. The authority of Jesus had been challenged constantly by the scribes and Pharisees. In fact, his power to work miracles had been attributed to demons. Then Jesus quotes Psalm 118,

> The stone the builders rejected
> has become the capstone;
> the Lord has done this,
> and it is marvelous in our eyes.

> Therefore I tell you that the kingdom of God will be taken away from you and given to a people who will produce its fruit. He who falls on this stone will be broken to pieces, but he on whom it falls will be crushed" (Matt. 21:42-44).

Let me give you still another perspective. Heaven without the clothes of righteousness would be the worst kind of hell. There are things in my life I am grateful that you do not know (though at my age my sins tend to bore most people). Still, I hide nothing from God. God sees me as I really am. Imagine my showing up at heaven's door unwashed by the blood of Jesus (God has given us the sacrificial righteousness of Jesus Christ as a wedding garment), presuming to plead my own case, with my sins hanging out, utterly exposed for the rest of eternity. John Wesley insisted that this would be a fate worse than fire and brimstone. In fact, Wesley took a line from some of the mystic writers and insisted that hell was the creation of God's love, not God's wrath. The mystics imagined our showing up in heaven, presuming to plead our own case, believing that our own righteous clothes were really quite adequate, thank you very much. Suddenly, God comes to welcome us to our new home, and, observing the misery of our nakedness, creates the darkness of hell to give such presumption a place to escape the awful exposure.

I recall an Andy Capp cartoon (the despicable little English sot is always getting drunk and chasing women). It seems on one occasion Andy is stumbling down the street only to pause long enough to pop a penny in the "Save Our Roof Fund" box attached to the door of the local parish vicarage. At that point the vicar comes out and says, "Thank you, Andy, you will go to heaven for that, *but you won't like it.*" Never mind the theology here, the point is that Andy would not like heaven because Andy could not bear the light. In order to "enjoy God forever" we must put on the wedding garment, the righteousness of God's son Jesus Christ.

**My Friend in Cornwall**

Shortening the leap does not always begin with Jesus, however. Honest doubt sometimes asks the question behind the question. I have a friend named Taff who claims to be an atheist (though in my opinion not a very good one). He lives in a small fishing village nestled in a cove on the English Channel in Cornwall, England, and is one of the few remaining small-boat fishermen along the southwestern coast. I've known Taff for almost ten years, visiting his village nearly every year for a week or so of rest and relaxation. His only perception of anything beyond the senses involves two unrelated experiences. One is to sit in his overstuffed chair with a glass of Scotch looking out his living room window at the reflection of the moon on a shimmering sea. The other is to remember the love of his father who was a fisherman along that same coast, who after he retired would climb the coastal path, sit on a boulder high above the sea and watch over his son as he fished alone in his boat far below. My friend believes that occasionally his father will suddenly appear on that boulder, still watching over him more than ten years after his death. The experience is sometimes so real that he blinks his eyes to see if the image can be sustained. The apparition of his father will sometimes remain there for hours. He once asked if I believed that possible. My response? Of course it's possible, but it takes faith to believe that your dad is still there watching over you after all these years. Without faith you would miss out on this wonderful experience altogether. He nodded. Then I said, "That is the same way with God. Without faith we can miss a heavenly Father who is watching over us as well." He tapped his head and said, "You got me thinking."

God appeared in Jesus to convince us that our heavenly Father watches over us as well. The seeds of faith are already at work and my task is simply to pray that God will give me the insight to cultivate that seed so that you, and people like Taff, can move from doubt to faith, from belief that the man Jesus not only lived, but died, that you might have life everlasting.

**End Notes**

[1] That is not to say that these challenges are not real. Certainly they are. James K.A. Smith's book, *Who's Afraid of Postmodernism?: Taking Derrida, Lyotard, and Foucault to Church* (Baker Academic, 2006) cites the July 15, 1972, demolition of the Pruitt-Ingoe housing development for low-income people in St. Louis (the so-called "machine for modern living" was deemed an uninhabitable environment), along with the 1968 student riots and the fall of the Berlin Wall as evidence of the collapse of modernity's naive attempts to solve the world's problems without striking the root.

[2] This and all other quotations from the Bible (unless otherwise noted) are from the *New International Version* (Zondervan Press).

[3] In fact (although there is no real evidence of this having taken place), every fifty years (during the year of Jubilee) all sold property should have reverted to the original owner (Lev. 25:8-55).

[4] Some commentators identify the scroll with a divine decree, God's ultimate will (see Craig Koester, *Revelation and the End of All Things*, pp. 76ff.).

[5] It should be said that some theology has no original good news (in effect, beginning with the "bad" news), so there is nothing to be restored to, while some theology has no bad news, so there is no need to be restored.

CHAPTER TWO

# "CAN GOD FORGIVE A SINNER LIKE ME?"

## (THE IMPORTANCE OF REPENTANCE AND FAITH)

I heard a comedian state on TV a few years ago, "The problem with you evangelical Christians is that you blame 9/11 on God. If that's true, then God's a prick."

Do we talk about God so that the world can possibly believe that God is a prick? God forgive us. No wonder honest doubt has difficulty believing that God can forgive. Just as our need to forgive will be highlighted in the next chapter, we first of all need to be forgiven. The question, "Can God forgive a sinner like me?" comes from a man who not only sinned, but who was reluctant to give up the sin that was consuming him. How do we respond to such a person? What of the role of repentance and faith?

### An Exchange of Letters

A couple of years ago a woman, whom I had met with her husband at a retreat center, wrote me a letter regarding her husband's infidelity. They were now estranged but she was praying for reconciliation. Could I help them?

I was swamped with the first days of a new semester, so I wrote back simply saying that I was truly sorry to hear about their problems but that I did not know what I could do (beyond small counsel) if her husband was not open to counsel as well. I then asked for her husband's address, promising to drop him a note (which I did) to say that I was available if he wanted someone to listen. I assumed that this was the end of the story since no marriage can be healed unilaterally. Then, this letter arrived from the husband.

> *Bob,*
>
> *I appreciate you taking the time to contact me regarding the situation that I find myself in. I do not know how much you know, but you are right in saying that we are working through some heavy stuff. To be honest, I may be losing my mind over this "stuff." For about six months now I have been seeing another woman whom I love.*
>
> *I no longer love my wife as I once did. She is a great person, a great mother and a wonderful Christian woman. Her faith is inspiring. Something happened between us that I cannot put my finger on that has made our relationship strained at best. It happened over time, perhaps years, and is to the point where I do not wish to try to work things out.*
>
> *Perhaps because of all that has gone on in my life in the past year or so, I have completely lost my relationship with God. I cannot pray effectively. I go to church to worship but feel like a fraud and hypocrite and usually end up leaving early so I do not have to talk*

*with anyone. Just over a year ago I thought I was supposed to be a pastor. Now I cannot imagine preaching God's Word. I know that I abandoned God, and I know that God is with me always. My first sermon was on the parables of Luke 15. I am now one of those lost sheep or coins. Why would God allow me to go astray? Why do I feel so disconnected? Is it possible to get back to a close relationship with God after a divorce? Am I destined for hell because of my leaving my wife for another woman? Can God forgive a sinner like me?*

*Please let me know what you think and what God's Word says that He has in store for sinners like me.*

*Thank you for your concern and willingness to help.*

You can imagine that after reading such a heartrending letter I took a good bit of time composing my response. Here is a copy (Bruce and Marsha are obviously not their real names).

*Dear Bruce,*

*I've been praying about this response—a lot. Thank you for your honesty and for your questions. I'm sure you realize that love (like many things) is a decision. You decide to go crazy. You decide not to go crazy (I've considered it a time or two myself). You decide to love Marsha. You decide not to love Marsha. I think what concerned me most about your comments was the statement, "Why would God allow me to go astray?" You know the answer to that, Bruce. The only other option is for God to force you into obedience, and the freedom of choice has always been integral to a vital relationship with a God who "first loved us," as a choice.*

*You describe yourself as one of the lost sheep or coins. You feel disconnected because of disobedience. You have said as much. Now you want God to say it is OK to divorce Marsha and marry this other woman. You ask if you are destined for hell when you are already in hell. That is what disobedience feels like. The hope is that you are still close enough to God so that you still feel guilty when you mess up. Heb. 12:6 says "the Lord disciplines those he loves," and God disciplines us primarily through our consciences. We start to die spiritually when we start to rationalize sin. Thank God you are not trying to rationalize sin.*

*One question you did not ask is if you and Marsha could ever have love renewed (I mean fall back in love with the woman you married)? I believe you can, and here is how: Break off the relationship with the other woman today—at least until the marriage issue is settled with Marsha. You owe Marsha and the kids that much. You owe the other woman that much. If she is worthy of you, she will not want a man who would take up with someone else before he had resolved a marriage with a "great person, a great mother and a wonderful Christian." You can decide to love Marsha. You may not feel it, but feeling comes with commitment. Beg Marsha to forgive you and let her ask your forgiveness as well (there are always two sides). Then commit to working on the marriage with some solid counseling. This is what that will do for you. Immediately you will have peace of mind. Immediately your relationship with God will be renewed, and you will begin to hear and learn new things from the Spirit of God. I believe that your call will be renewed and you can spend the rest of your life offering hope to others who suffer similar experiences.*

*Listen, my friend, you are a good man who wants to do what is right. That is so clear to me. Your integrity, your life, your ministry, your family, your children are at stake. If you pray about this, we both know what God will say. Thank God for a woman like Marsha who loves you enough to forgive you (that is a rare find, believe me). I'm telling you that love can be renewed. Please turn this thing around before you do something you will regret for the rest of your life. You can do this. You really can. I know you feel like you have gone too far, but that is a lie from the enemy. Obey God and you can have the peace that you want so badly before you go to bed tonight. God will help you. Trust him.*

*I'm not asking you to deny the feelings you have for this other woman. Those are real. I'm simply asking you to realize that the consequences of what you are thinking about doing are even more real—for everyone concerned.*

*I'm reminded of a text, "If they have escaped the corruption of the world by knowing our Lord and Savior Jesus Christ and are again entangled in it and overcome, they are worse off at the end than they were at the beginning" (II Peter 2:20). Know that I love you, Bruce. I'm committed to pray for you every day until this thing is resolved, one way or the other. In the meantime, please know that I remain,*

*Your real friend,*

**The Rest of the Story**

I wish I had good news to report on this situation. I do not. Though Bruce never wrote me back, if I could write a follow-up letter today, this is what I would say.

*Dear Bruce,*

*I heard recently that you and Marsha are now divorced and you have married "the other woman." Let me address one of the questions you asked in that woeful letter of some years back, "Can God forgive a sinner like me?" Not only can God forgive a sinner like you, but God also delights in forgiving sinners like you and can even renew that call upon your life to Christian ministry. God wants to fill you afresh with the Holy Spirit.*

*You might recall from my presentation at the retreat center that the Hebrew word for wind is* ruah, *translated in the Greek by the word* pneuma, *spirit. Why would the word for spirit translate the word for wind? It is because that is no accidental metaphor. Meteorologists tell us that wind moves from high pressure to low pressure, to the point of least resistance. Since I live part of the time in Florida I know lots about low pressure. You don't have to convince wind to move from high pressure to low pressure; that's what wind does, sometimes at speeds of nearly 200 miles per hour. Similarly, you don't have to convince Spirit to move from high pressure to low pressure; that's what Spirit does. So, how do we create low pressure so we can be filled with the Holy Spirit and empowered for the future? The key is repentance and faith. Let me explain.*

*First of all, what is repentance? Most commentaries go to the Greek word* metanoia, *which literally translates, "to turn around." That can be misleading if we exegete the word and not the image behind the word, especially if one gets the impression that in order to repent I must somehow turn my back on sin. You wish. Just try to turn your back on sin by trying to turn your back on sin. It will consume you. For that matter, just try to take your mind off sin by trying to take your mind off sin. The split second your mind goes rote you have thoughts in the middle of the Lord's Prayer. Repentance is not turning your back on sin. If you could do that, you would not need God. Repentance is grieving over the separation that your sin has caused to the place where you can pray this simple prayer. "God, as far as I know my own heart, I am willing for you to take from me anything that is separating me from you, myself, and those around me. I now want to renew my faith and trust in your Son Jesus Christ at the point of that repentance." Swoosh. That creates low pressure and the Holy Spirit moves to the very ground of your being, bringing forgiveness and the power to go and sin no more.*

*So, what is faith? Faith, according to Hebrews 11:1 "is being sure of what we hope for and certain of what we do not see." To put it another way, it is committing all that we know of ourselves to all that we know of God so that the Spirit of God can bear witness with our spirits that we are children of God (Rom. 8:16). It is trusting God to be true to all of the biblical promises.*

*I mentioned in my first letter to you that Hebrews 12 insists that God disciplines those whom God loves. How? Primarily through our consciences, we feel guilty when we mess up so that we cannot rationalize our sin. I mentioned then that we start to die spiritually when we start to rationalize sin. So, guilt is a good thing, but if we do not get beyond the guilt, it quickly turns to condemnation, and that's a bad thing. I don't want your guilt to turn to condemnation. At some point we all need to repent and receive God's forgiveness and receive the power to get on with our lives. Romans 8:1-4 states that*

> There is now no condemnation for those who are in Christ Jesus, because through Christ Jesus the law of the Spirit of life set me free from the law of sin and death. For what the law was powerless to do in that it was weakened by the sinful nature, God did by sending his own Son in the likeness of sinful man to be a sin offering. And so he condemned sin in sinful man, in order that the righteous requirements of the law might be fully met in us, who do not live according to the sinful nature but according to the Spirit.

*You once preached a sermon on the parable of the lost sheep and lost coin. Do you remember what happened when the sheep and the coin were found? The owners rejoiced! Please know that as you repent and renew your faith and trust in Jesus Christ, God welcomes you back and all heaven rejoices. I rejoice as well.*

*In closing, may I say that my last letter to you might have seemed harsh and inflexible? Please know that at that moment I was trying to speak words of reconciliation for you and Marsha. Now, however, since you have moved on and are remarried, may I wish you and your new wife all the best in your marriage. I pray you will have a wonderful life together and that you will hear and receive a new call upon your life for Christian ministry (either as a pastor or a layperson). In the meantime, please believe that I still remain,*

*Your real friend,*

### The Nature of God's Forgiveness

Decisions to answer God's call are usually a process of "leaps" along the way. One of those leaps must involve asking for and receiving God's forgiveness. Where my friend is concerned, there comes a time to move from feeling to fact in order to counter the disillusionments of the past. Feeling frequently sustains the weight of condemnation. Fact speaks the word of truth that God's forgiveness is available to those who repent and believe. Although forgiveness is not *unconditional*, it is *constant* and *habitual*. Jesus said, "If your brother sins, rebuke him, and *if he repents*, forgive him" (Luke 17:3).

Forgiveness is conditional in the sense that we must repent (we must grieve over the separation our sin has caused and be willing for God to take it from us as we renew our faith and trust in God's provision, Jesus Christ). Forgiveness is constant and habitual in the sense that it is always available. Short of death, there is no statute of limitations, no date of expiration. Jesus also said, "If he sins against you *seven times in a day*, and seven times comes back to you and says, 'I repent,' *forgive him*" (Luke 17:4).

Would God ask us to do something that God had not already clearly demonstrated? The words of Jesus on the cross, "Father, forgive them, for they do not know what they are doing" (Luke 23:34), illustrate this profoundly and unmistakably. This is not to excuse those responsible. In fact, all of us are responsible since "all have sinned and fall short of the glory of God" (Rom. 3:23). This is to remind us of the significance of the Cross.

**The Covenant and the Cross**

The concept of the Old Testament covenant connected the forgiveness of sin with the shedding of blood (Heb. 9:22). In effect, *the conditions of that earlier covenant ultimately lead to the necessity of the Cross.* For years my students would ask, "Why speak so much about covenant? It makes God seem so bloodthirsty." Then it dawned. God did not invent the concept of covenant. That was already in place. Biblical scholars tell us that in Abraham's day it was common practice to establish a relationship through the cutting of covenant. An animal was divided and the two parties passed between the halves of the animal vowing that if either party betrayed the covenant, might the same fate befall them. Biblical theologians may have difficulty establishing a historical Abraham but the concept of covenant can be documented beyond question.[1] God relates to Abraham in a way that Abraham could understand. Furthermore, the need for sacrifice to renew that covenant was God's way of underscoring the seriousness of sin. Sin is costly. It separates and will cost you a sacrifice without blemish. Don't give God your one-eyed goat! Only your best will do.

Certainly, God could have redeemed us from the Fall in any number of ways but chose the Cross as a new and better way. The old covenant was established with the blood of bulls and goats but these were unable to clear the conscience, to remove the weight of condemnation (Heb. 9:9). That would take a new covenant, not made with human hands, eternal in the heavens, requiring a human sacrifice without blemish. Since before creation the importance of that sacrifice had been established and those directly responsible for crucifying Jesus had no idea the significance of their act ("they do not know what they are doing"). Satan overplayed his hand (he tends to do that). He should have never touched the boy. One of the most telling scenes in the movie *The Passion* is the screaming, cowering character portraying Satan when Jesus died and the veil in the Temple was rent from top to bottom. Suddenly through faith in what Jesus had done on the cross, planet earth once again had access to the very presence of God. Forgiveness was available to all who would repent and believe.

My friend "Bruce" is testimony that one can experience the pangs of hell long before physical death. I pray that he has received the forgiveness of God and experienced a foretaste of heaven so that he can get on with his life and ministry.

Today there was a story on the news of a prominent minister admitting to sin. I'm sorry. I'm even embarrassed for him and the church, but it happens. Do we cast him aside? Some say that the Christian army is the only army in the world that slays it's own wounded. What does God say to this "fallen" brother? *If you repent, I will forgive you that you might forgive others.*

The prodigal returns, the lost sheep is found, the coin is recovered, all heaven rejoices and the world is a better place.

**End Notes**

[1] The only possible extra-biblical evidence for Abraham that is fairly widely accepted is in the topographical list of the Egyptian Pharaoh Shoshenq I (c. 925, nos. 71 & 72), giving what may be read as "The Enclosure of Abram" (see K.A. Kitchen, On the Reliability of the Old Testament, Eerdmans, 2003). The concept of covenant, however, can be confirmed time and again throughout the Nuzi and Mari tablets. For the first couple of decades after their discovery, a consensus emerged that the tablets firmly established the patriarchal period as a historical fact of the first half of the second millennium B.C. and that the parallels between the Nuzi documents and the Mari materials suggest that the custom of cutting covenants detailed in Genesis was common practice throughout the period in question.

CHAPTER THREE

# "HOW CAN I FORGIVE?"
## (CONFRONTING THE PAST)

If I had to name only a few of the driving forces that threaten people in this generation (especially since 9/11), one would have to be our need to forgive. I've seen condemnation fuel honest doubt, not only when we fail to receive forgiveness, but also when we fail to forgive others. Many of us carry deep-seated resentments. They control us at every level of our lives. William Faulkner once said, "The past is never dead, it's not even past." I know a woman who was terribly abused by her now dead father. "How can I forgive someone already in the grave? He still controls my life."

How can any of us overcome such things? We live in a world where an "eye for an eye" seems to rule. Many of my Muslim friends have a need for revenge that never goes away until retribution is complete (Surah 2:194).[1] The Bible says,

"Do not take revenge, my friends, but leave room for God's wrath, for it is written: 'It is mine to avenge; I will prepay,' says the LORD" (Rom. 12:19). Jesus taught that the Holy Spirit enables you to release such resentment so that you can get on with your life.

After several months of counseling with my abused friend, I suggested that she write her father a letter and simply place it on his grave. I was humbled and grateful when she came back the next week believing that she had somehow been delivered, in that instant. Is that a mind thing, or a God thing? Perhaps both, but God was at work.

**Loving Our Neighbors as We Love Ourselves**

Lest you think this kind of abuse is an isolated incident, sociologists tell us that nearly forty percent of us were somehow abused as children. I recently spent an evening with a former judge who was (for nearly thirty years) an advocate for abused children. He tells me that the effects of such abuse are devastating and long lasting. Do you have any idea how difficult it is to believe that God loves you if you were abused as a child? Let me give you a principle. *If you do not know that God loves you, you do not love yourself, and if you do not love yourself, you don't love anyone.* The Gospels tell us that the greatest commandment is to "Love the Lord your God with all your heart and with all your soul and with all your mind and with all your strength. The second is this, 'Love your neighbor as yourself.' There is no commandment greater than these" (Mk. 12:31; cf. Mt. 19:19 & Lk. 10:27).

A student came into class not too long ago with a story. He was in a coffee bar attempting to witness to a new acquaintance. At one point he said something to the effect that "God loves you, and I love you." The acquaintance immediately reacted, "How can you say you love me, you don't even know me?" My student replied, "God tells me to love my neighbor as I love myself, and I love myself—a lot!"

Nearly thirty-five years ago I had an experience that changed my life forever. I was living in Pasadena, California, where I was beginning a teaching career. I was also struggling with some personal issues. Somewhat overwhelmed I felt myself slipping into depression. One morning, as I was jogging around the Rose Bowl, I remember asking God a question. "God, do you still love me?" Thinking probably not, imagine my surprise when I sensed this reply, "Tuttle, don't you know why I love you? I don't love you because I'm a God of love, though I am; and I don't love you because that's what I do best, though it is; and I don't love you because I'm supposed to, though I am. The reason I love you is, there's just something about you that flat out turns me on!" Whoa! Suddenly my name was no longer Legion! I was healed in an instant. I was running on air. Then, it hit me. There was something about me that God simply adored. God was not only my Savior; God was my forever friend. Then (perhaps for the very first time), I understood the principle. If I'm good enough for God, I ought to be good enough for you. What do you think of that? Furthermore, if *you* are good enough for God, you ought to be good enough for those around you. What do you think of that? Perhaps most important of all, if *you* are good enough for God, you ought to be good enough for *yourself*. So what do you think of that?

Loving yourself is not the self-centered kind of love that puts *you* at the center of the universe. Loving yourself is realizing that God loves you to the point where God delights in who you are and is eager to use you as an instrument of grace for affecting positive change in the hearts and lives of others.

Obviously the point of all this is that if you love yourself, you fall in love with others. Furthermore, love is quick to forgive and forgiveness inevitably turns into compassion for others.

## Releasing Deep-Seated Resentments

My wife and I have a favorite text. It is Luke 6:37-38.

> Do not judge, and you will not be judged. Do not condemn, and you will not be condemned. Forgive, and you will be forgiven. Give, and it will be given to you. A good measure, pressed down, shaken together and running over, will be poured into your lap. For with the measure you use, it will be measured to you.

Let me be brutally honest. Some of you have every right to hold resentments. Philip Yancey tells this story.

> The church I attend reserves a brief time in which people in the pews can voice aloud their prayers. Over the years, I have heard hundreds of these prayers, and with very few exceptions, the word *polite* applies. One, however, stands out in my memory because of its raw emotion.
>
> In a clear but wavering voice, a young woman began with the words, "God, I hated you after the rape! How could you let this happen to me?" The congregation abruptly fell silent. No more rustling of papers or shifting in seats. "And I hated the people in this church who tried to comfort me. I didn't want comfort. I wanted revenge. I wanted to hurt back. I thank you, God, that you didn't give up on me and neither did some of these people. You kept after me, and I come back to you now and ask that you heal the scars in my soul."[2]

Need I tell you that the Bible is replete with such prayers, especially from some of God's favorite daughters and sons such as Abraham, Moses, Hannah and David. Nearly half the Psalms, for example, yield to this outline: They

- Thank God for past mercies (read Psalm 21).
- Make an appeal to God on the basis of the

author's own righteousness. What! David, who broke nearly every commandment, makes an appeal on the basis of his own righteousness? In effect, David seems to be saying, "God, I may not be perfect but I'm giving it my best shot. You got me into this mess, you had better see me through it" (read Psalm 17).
- Confess sins. This is really important (read Psalm 51).
- Anticipate a blessing from God (read Psalm 23).

Then, there is the book of Job. The end of that story gives added meaning to "good measure, pressed down, shaken together and running over." I know many of you have been horribly mistreated and, in some instances, the mistreatment continues. I do not blame you for feeling as you do, but, *if you are not willing for God to take this resentment from you, that gives this person just that much more power over you, and that always creates issues of self-worth* . . . . We established in an earlier chapter that you cannot give your sin to God. If you could give your sin to God, you would not need God. The principle remains. If you are grieving over the separation the resentment has caused and are willing for God to take it from you as you renew your faith and trust in Jesus Christ at the point of that repentance, the Holy Spirit comes into your life and does the work for you. I've tested this principle a hundred times. It works. It really does.

### A Brand Plucked from the Burning

Despair is the tool of the Accuser. Just this morning I was reading in Zechariah where Zechariah is admonishing the Jews who have returned from exile to complete the rebuilding of the temple in Jerusalem. Suddenly Zechariah had a vision of

> ... Joshua the high priest standing before the angel of the LORD, and Satan standing at his right side to accuse him. The LORD said to Satan, "The LORD rebuke you, Satan! The LORD, who has chosen Jerusalem, rebuke you! Is not this man a burning stick snatched from the fire?" (Zech. 3:1-2).

Those who know the life of John Wesley will remember the words, "brand plucked from the burning," as a reference to this verse and applied to the small boy, John, by his mother, Susanna, following his narrow escape from a fire at the Epworth rectory set by "the enemies of God." Later in life John Wesley would recall these words as he recounted another narrow escape, this time from a life of self-righteousness. An evangelist plucked from the burning.

I have a print by Rembrandt, "The Return of the Prodigal Son" hanging over a prayer bench in my office. Here the son is kneeling before his father and in his father's full embrace while the elder son (and others) stands to the side, watching. The original painting hangs in the Hermitage Museum in St. Petersburg, Russia. I once stood before that masterpiece for thirty minutes, in silent prayer. God is that kind of a father. I know it's true. I can feel it in my bones.[3] The prodigal plucked from the burning.

Last year I published a book, *The Story of Evangelism*. At one point I tell the story of Monica, the mother of Augustine of Hippo. Monica prayed for and then pursued her wayward son throughout the Roman Empire until she found him secure under the influence of Ambrose of Milan, who plunged him into the waters of baptism on Easter Eve. There is something about the tenacity of a mother's love that pursues, directs, and then releases her children to the next generation. The Apostle Paul writes,

> As apostles of Christ we could have been a burden

to you, but we were gentle among you, like a mother caring for her little children. We loved you so much that we were delighted to share with you not only the gospel of God but our lives as well.

God is that kind of a mother. I know it's true. I can feel it in my bones. A saint plucked from the burning.

Forgiveness is a consistent theme in the teachings of Jesus. The story of the woman caught in adultery is just as well known as that of the prodigal. When the woman is brought before Jesus "as a trap, in order to have a basis for accusing him" (John 8:6), Jesus bends down and apparently begins doodling on the ground. As the Pharisees continued to press him, finally he straightens up and says, "If any one of you is without sin, let him be the first to throw a stone at her" (v. 7). He then stoops once again and this time apparently begins to write with purpose and intent. At this they all go away, beginning with the oldest.

"Woman, where are they? Has no one condemned you? . . . Then neither do I condemn you . . . . Go now and leave your life of sin" (vv.10-11). A woman plucked from the burning.

I John 4:4 gives us the perspective, "You, dear children, are from God and have overcome them [evil spirits], because the One who is in you is greater than the one who is in the world." The people of God, plucked from the burning.

### The Nature of Our Forgiveness

A high priest, John Wesley, the prodigal, a saint, an adulterous woman and the people of God all teach us that there is a spirit of forgiveness that is quick to be reconciled, to refresh and renew. It is accompanied by a change of attitude toward the offending person from negative to positive. As with all of the above, it is not quick to condemn. In fact, our first reaction should always be to forgive as a disposition of mind and spirit. After all, we have been forgiven (Matt. 6:12, 14-15; 18:21-35).

Our forgiveness does NOT, however, imply *pardon*—who

has the power to pardon? It does NOT *condone* as a means of justifying the offense. It does NOT *excuse*, as if the offender were helpless to sin. It does NOT *forget*—who can forget? It does NOT *deny*, as if the offense never really happened.

Our forgiveness IS, however—as a disposition of mind and spirit—relentless in its willingness to release the resentment to a loving and forgiving God who is willing to take it from us the moment we are willing to be delivered.

I'm reading a book, *Blood Brothers*, by Elias Chacour, a Palestinian Christian whose family was displaced by Zionists during Israel's struggle to establish a nation after 1948. Although the Israeli government was officially more tolerant of it's Arab brothers and sisters who had lived on those lands for thousands of years, many of the soldiers in the north were cruel and uncompromising. Not only were Arab lands confiscated and then sold to "well-to-do" settlers (as some sort of investment), but also their homes were destroyed. Elias, the ten-year-old son, thinks to himself when the news is received that they are now hopelessly homeless. He grieves, especially for his father who must watch the fig orchard that he planted with such tenderness and affection now carelessly tended by someone else. His father had strained with heavy clay jars of water up the steep slopes, caring for each sapling as if it were one of his own children until it was strong enough to survive on its own. In the same moment he wishes that his father would rage, but then is terrified that his dear gentle father, in such agony of spirit, would weep.

When he spoke in a few minutes, his voice was barely above a whisper.

"Children," he said softly, turning those sad eyes upon us, "if someone hurts you, you can curse him. But this would be useless. Instead, you have to ask the Lord to bless the man who makes himself your enemy. And do you know what will happen? The Lord will bless you with inner peace—and perhaps your enemy will turn from his wickedness. If not, the Lord will deal with him."[4]

Is there someone whom you need to forgive? Is there someone who needs your forgiveness? Are there whole peoples whom you need to forgive? Are there whole peoples who need your forgiveness?

The picture at the head of this chapter captures the destruction of the twin towers in New York City on 9/11/2001. What would it mean for Americans to forgive the terrorist cells responsible for such wanton destruction? Can justice be served and forgiveness available at the same moment? Can the guilty be brought to trial and imprisoned and the deep-seated resentments be released at the same time? That may be our greatest challenge, but our only hope.

Do we understand the hatred that leads to such acts of violence? Are we somehow partially to blame? Can something be done to defuse such hatred in the future so that our children and grandchildren can live in a kinder, gentler and safer world? What if we took the words of Jesus literally (which I'm convinced was his intent)?

> Forgive us our debts, as we also have forgiven our debtors . . . . For if you forgive men when they sin against you, your heavenly Father will also forgive you. But if you do not forgive men their sins, your Father will not forgive your sins (Matt. 6:12-15).

Swallow hard. Those are some of the earliest words recorded in the ministry of Jesus. Does our willingness to forgive begin with God's forgiveness of us, or is it the other way around? Does God's forgiveness begin with our forgiveness of others? Either way, forgiveness is the key and the Spirit of God is ready to deliver. Let God arise.

**End Notes**

[1] The *Qur'an* speaks of the Law of *Qisas* or retaliation. Surah 2:194 reads, "All sacred things are (under the law) retaliation; whoever acts aggressively against you, inflict injury on him according to the injury he has inflicted on you . . . ." (Translated by M.H. Shakir, Tahrike Tarsile Qur'an, Inc.). All subsequent quotations from the *Qur'an* are from this same translation.

[2] Philip Yancey, posted on his website 10/20/2006.

[3] In fact, Henri Nouwen's book, *The Return of the Prodigal Son*, speaks of a similar experience after sitting for several hours before that same painting.

[4] Elias Chacour, *Blood Brothers: A Palestinian's Struggle for Reconciliation in the Middle East*, Kingsway Publication, 1984, p. 62.

CHAPTER FOUR

# "How Can I Overcome?"
## (The universal question)

This photo is of a nineteenth-century war memorial; a soldier is dying for what proved to be a lost cause. Some years ago I circled the globe with these questions in mind: "Are there transcultural common denominators that communicate with more or less equal effectiveness in every culture? Are there questions that honest doubt asks on a global scale?" I came back with several responses, but the key that turned the lock was that everyone the world over has a need to measure up to some form of law.[1] Furthermore, we found that when people were serious about such a law, they had become frustrated with their inability to measure up and were asking questions about accessing a power that would enable them to overcome. That is what Christianity is all about. Put the tenets of the Christian faith into principles of supply and demand, and the demand is out there. It is universal, and the supply is endless.

**Email Correspondence with an Airplane Companion**

Just over two years ago I was seated in the exit row of an airplane (that gives me a bit more legroom). As we were taking off a man with a long tall frame was seated just behind me. He was miserable (I could feel his knees pressing against the back of my seat). Since the space next to me was empty, when the seatbelt sign was turned off I leaned around and invited him to join me. He was grateful and we began to chat. I soon learned that though he made more money in a year than I would make in the next four he was so consumed that he had never owned a passport and had not read a book in ten years. He complained that there was just no one to hold him accountable. I told him that if he liked, I would write to him just a sentence or two a month until he owned a passport and had read at least one book. He seemed grateful, so I kept in touch.

Six months later he informed me that he was now the proud owner of a passport and that he had read the *Chronicles of Narnia* to his daughters. We continued to write just one or two sentences a month for the next eighteen months.

Then, on one occasion, he wrote, "If you are ever in my part of the country I would like to come and hear you speak."

When I wrote back that I was to be in his state in just a few weeks, he replied, "Unfortunately we are about four hours or so from there, and I don't have much time to get away. I hope your speaking engagement goes well. What is the topic?"

I responded with my usual sentence or two, "The topic is the person and work of the Holy Spirit (accessing the power of God to overcome the stuff that would attempt to swallow us). Make sense?" Then I received this:

## Chapter 4: "How Can I Overcome?"

*Bob,*
*Actually, I would like to ask your advice as I respect you so much.*

*Here is a problem of mine: I have a part of my personality that is not very pleasant, and I have to try very hard to make a change in my behavior. Specifically, when I argue on a subject with my wife or kids or other acquaintance, I can become overbearing and anxious to get my point across at the expense of appreciating the other side's issues and feelings. When I have one of these episodes, I look back at the event and realize that I can be very unpleasant and downright disrespectful. I want to have more control over my emotions and my style of communicating at these times. My intentions are good, but I speak and act in a way that I'm not proud of in those certain heated debates.*

*I can't even measure the love I have for my wife and my family, and I have a very wonderful and loving home environment and we are truly happy with a capital "H." There are just these occasional arguments that escalate, and I'm primarily to blame for not allowing a difference of opinion or even simple perspective!*

*I have the motivation, but in the heat of the moment, my willingness to change seems non-existent, and I continue to be disrespectful when I get heavily involved in an argument that I feel strongly about. I am very passionate about certain things, but I lose my balance in the approach and words and manner!!*

*What do you suggest that can give me more power to be respectful and calm when these situations arise? How can I overcome?*

My response was immediate:

*Dear Brother,*
*I've been thinking and praying about your last message. You realize that I'm an old man, so life is too short to mince words. First of all, you have incredible insight into your own problem. Most people with that problem do not see it. Secondly, you have the motivation to change. We are already almost there. Thirdly, some*

*of your attitude has to do with perspective, and that can be easily corrected. Finally, the ultimate solution will come from on High and that is where I can help you the most.*

*Let's look first of all at perspective. Is being right more important than communicating love and understanding? You obviously think not. The biggest learning experience for me over the years was to graduate from my need to be right to an awareness of God's Spirit as the operative power in this age, so that I began to bend my efforts toward developing receivers for God's still small voice. Let me give you an example. I'm driving down the freeway and I see someone coming up behind me at a high rate of speed who will try to cut in front of me as I approach another car. Do I speed up so that there will be no room, or do I back off and let them get on by? I've decided to use my automobile as a ministry. Instead of getting angry I try to look for opportunities to bless people simply by cutting them enough slack so they can get on with their busy lives. I cannot tell you what that has done for me. I am no longer angry, defensive or discourteous. I can actually encourage people into believing that someone out there is not out to get them. This morning I let a truck into my line of traffic on a busy highway and for half a mile he kept waving and thanking me.*

*Let me give you another perspective. You are tall. When tall people get argumentative it is always overkill. You are big enough and strong enough to be gentle. Remember, we put the pressure on by taking the pressure off. My wife always gets to me by saying, "Sweetheart, you may be right." I'm always looking for opportunities to repay that compliment.*

*Now the crunch. Here is how to access the power to change. The Apostle Paul writes,*

> Since we have been justified through faith, we have peace with God through our Lord Jesus Christ, through whom we have gained access by faith into this grace in which we now stand. And we rejoice in the hope of the glory of God. Not only so, but

we also rejoice in our sufferings, because we know that suffering produces perseverance; perseverance, character; and character hope. And hope does not disappoint us, because God has poured out his love into our hearts by the Holy Spirit, whom he has given us (Rom. 5:1-5).

*Christians believe that the Holy Spirit is available to change our attitudes toward God, ourselves, and those around us (in fact, sin is that which separates us from God, ourselves and those around us, and if it is not separating us from God, ourselves, and those around us, we need not worry about it). It works something like this: The New Testament says that through repentance and faith the same power of the Holy Spirit available to Jesus and the disciples is available to us today. I don't mean this to sound magical, and I don't want you to take offense, but let me invite you to pray this prayer. "God, as far as I know my own heart I am willing for you to take this overbearing and anxious spirit from me. I cannot give it to you. If I could give it to you, I would not need you. I am, however, willing for you to take it from me as I place my faith and trust in your son Jesus, who died and rose that I might be the man you want me to be—for my family, for my business acquaintances, for all your creation. Amen."*

*My Brother, this is what happens. God calls that prayer repentance and faith, and the power of the Holy Spirit moves to the very ground of your being so that the next time you are tempted, your first reaction will be to resist the temptation. It will be easier to obey God than to disobey God, easier to resist the temptation than to yield to it. Now, listen. If you screw up (most of our sin is knee-jerk; we don't even think about it; it just happens to be the right time of the week), renew your repentance and faith and I promise you, you will get greater and greater distance on those things that would attempt to control you.*

*Does this make sense? I look forward to your response. In the meantime, know that I am praying for my young airplane companion and would appreciate your praying for me as God brings me to mind. Tonight I speak to 200-300 high school students after a football game in a town where I am speaking for the weekend. Help! I wish you were here to help me. Bob*

And the follow-up a few days later:

*Dear Bob,*
*I am thankful and appreciative that you took the time really to provide some insight. I've read your response several different times so that I could take from it as much as possible. Don't ever think that you could offend me. It's not possible because I know what's in your heart. In fact, let me apologize for not responding more quickly. The way my weeks go, I have these little moments in time to reflect/think/write and sometimes, those moments don't come around until I've missed the opportunity to be timely. But you and what you wrote to me have been on my mind. It is very important to me. In fact, I want to ask you (without bothering you for your time) to further explain one important thing you said. You used an example to help, but I'm still wondering about this:*
*"The biggest learning experience for me over the years was to graduate from the need of being right to an awareness of God's Spirit as the operative power in this age so that I began to bend my efforts toward developing receivers for God's still small voice."*
*Just last night, I had an opportunity to be better in a conversation . . . and I was . . . and I can tell I will improve over time.*
*And by the way, one of the best compliments I've ever had was your introduction to the last email: "Dear Brother." You reached out to me in the first two words in such a wonderful way by calling me your brother. The feeling is mutual!!!!*
*I hope all your travels and engagements go well.*

My response:

*Brother, I'm so proud of you. Now let me try to explain this:*

*The biggest learning experience for me over the years was to graduate from the need of being right to an awareness of God's Spirit as the operative power in this age so that I began to bend my efforts toward developing receivers for God's still small voice.*

*Many Christians think that if we can just believe the right stuff that everything will fall into place. As I mature (grow old) I'm beginning to realize that Christianity is more than that. God wants to be known and is constantly looking for ways of getting our attention. In fact, God has more invested in our lives than we do. The Bible teaches that the Spirit of God is also at work in the lives of those around us (our families, our colleagues, our friends, perhaps even our enemies), preparing them for our ministry (our attempts to bless them in any way we can). I tell my students that ninety percent of ministry is showing up and paying attention. I'm trying to pay better attention to what is going on around me. Where is God already at work in my sphere of influence? What is God saying to me as I read the Bible, as I pray, as I prepare my lectures, as I communicate with family, students and friends? I am always amazed at what God is teaching me. It makes life so much more interesting and a lot more fun.*

*Does that help? Keep on asking questions. I really like that. It means you are thinking. Bless you, my Brother. Our paths will cross again. In the meantime, please know that I remain, your real friend,*

## Overcoming...

Need I tell you that my airplane companion and I still correspond regularly? He has sent me photos of a trip abroad. He is overcoming; he really is. It occurs to me that the word "overcome" is the Apostle John's favorite word. We've already seen it in his insistence that "You, dear children, are from God and have overcome... because the One who is in you is greater than the one who is in the world" (I John 4:4). Follow that with

> Everyone who believes that Jesus is the Christ is born of God, and everyone who loves the father loves his child as well. This is how we know that we love the children of God: by loving God and carrying out his commands. This is love for God: to obey his commands. And his commands are not burdensome, for everyone born of God *overcomes* the world. This is the victory that has *overcome* the world, even our faith. Who is it that *overcomes* the world? Only he who believes that Jesus is the Son of God (I John 5:1-5).

Note the logic here. Those who place their faith and trust in Jesus Christ as God's provision for the forgiveness of sins are born of the Spirit and empowered to love God and obey God's commands. Furthermore, God's commands are not burdensome, for everyone born of God overcomes the world. Suddenly, we see our neighbors as God sees them, as we see our own children. Compassion rules "because God has poured out his love into our hearts by the Holy Spirit, whom he has given us" (Rom. 5:5).

The Apostle John is not yet through with the word "overcome," however. Chapters two and three of Revelation include letters to the seven churches of Asia, and every one of those letters turns on the word "overcome." In Ephesus, "To him who *overcomes*, I will give the right to eat from the tree of life…" (2:7). In Smyrna, "He who *overcomes* will not be hurt at all by the second death" (2:11). In Pergamum, "To him who *overcomes*, I will give some of the hidden manna" (2:17). In Thyatira, "To him who *overcomes* and does my will to the end, I will give authority over the nations" (2:26). In Sardis, "He who *overcomes* will, like them, be dressed in white. I will never blot out his name from the book of life, but will acknowledge his name before my Father and his angels" (3:4-

5). In Philadelphia, "Him who *overcomes* I will make a pillar in the temple of my God. Never again will he leave it" (3:11-12). In Laodicea, "To him who *overcomes*, I will give the right to sit with me on my throne, *just as I overcame* and sat down with my Father on his throne" (3:21).

That last phrase is especially significant. "Just as I overcame" implies that we will overcome as Christ himself overcame. That gives new meaning to "I am the vine; you are the branches. If a man remains in me and I in him, he will bear much fruit; apart from me you can do nothing…. If you remain in me and my words remain in you, ask whatever you wish, and it will be given you" (John 15:5, 7).

We do ministry by the way we view people. How do we view unchurched peoples? How do they view us? How do they view God? What are they looking for and how can we engage them so that they can understand just what's at stake.

More and more I am viewing people as HALT. Those of you in AA recognize that as an acrostic standing for **h**urting, **a**ngry, **l**onely and **t**ired. It is also the word used in the King James Bible to translate the Greek word for "lame" (John 5:3). The Navajo Indians have an expression, "Always assume that your visitor is hungry, lonely and tired." I find that when I see people as HALT I am far more compassionate and caring, and that, in itself, goes a long way toward having the mind of Christ Jesus.

> Who, being in very nature God,
> did not consider equality with God something to be grasped,
> but made himself nothing,
> taking the very nature of a servant,
> being made in human likeness.
> And being found in appearance as a man,
> he humbled himself
> and became obedient to death—
> even death on a cross! (Phil. 2:6-8)

One more story will close out this chapter. In Mark 9 we find a man whose son has a mute spirit but the disciples were unable to drive that spirit out of him. When the man brought the boy to Jesus, Jesus asked,

> "How long has he been like this?"
> "From childhood, . . . if you can do anything, take pity on us and help us. . . ."
> "'If you can'?" said Jesus. "Everything is possible for him who believes."
> Immediately the boy's father exclaimed, "I do believe, help me overcome my unbelief!"
> "You deaf mute spirit," he said, "I command you, come out of him and never enter him again. The spirit shrieked, convulsed him violently and came out."

"Help me overcome my unbelief," is a prayer that most of us have prayed on occasion, especially when something seems just too big. May I remind you that apart from the vine we can do nothing? The next time you see your neighbor suffering, apparently overwhelmed by her inability to overcome, pray believing that Jesus will enable you to speak a timely word or provide a needed service, and then bring others to pick up where you leave off and win the day to the glory of God.

My friend and church consultant, George Callendine, occasionally sends me some of his favorite quotations. Last week I received three of his best regarding prayer.[2]

Philip Yancey writes, "I used to worry about my deficiency of faith. My attitude is changing, though, as I begin to understand faith as a form of *engagement* with God. I may not be able to summon up belief in miracles or dream big dreams, but I can indeed exercise my faith by engaging with God in prayer." I like that.

Archbishop Richard Trench insists that "prayer is not overcoming God's reluctance, it is laying hold of God's highest willingness."

Follow that thought with the words of E. M. Bounds: "Prayer in its highest form and grandest success assumes the attitude of a wrestler with God." Surely, our desperate outbursts hardly threaten God, sometimes they even seem to change the mind of the One who loves us most. When God threatens to destroy "a stiff-necked people" who have built a golden calf, Moses pleads,

> Turn from your fierce anger; relent and do not bring disaster on your people. Remember your servants Abraham, Isaac and Israel, to whom you swore by your own self: "I will make your descendants as numerous as the stars in the sky and I will give your descendants all this land I promised them, and it will be their inheritance forever." *Then the LORD relented and did not bring on his people the disaster he had threatened* (Emphasis mine Ex. 32:12-14).

How many times does God apparently relent when the saints pray? Not all the time, but sometimes God would appear to listen to the heartened pleas of those who simply refuse to give up. God delights in persistence. Be encouraged. Faith believes that help is on the way and could well be just around the corner.

CHAPTER FIVE

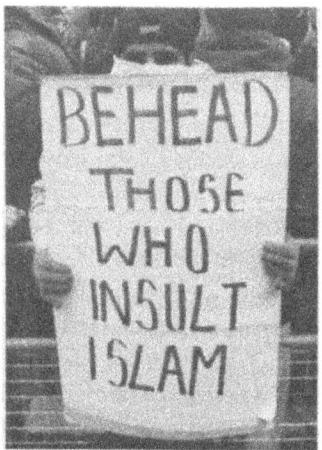

# "WHAT ABOUT THE OTHER RELIGIONS OF THE WORLD?"

(HAVE YOU READ THE QUR'AN LATELY?)

Most honest doubt finds pause in the fact that hundreds of millions of perfectly wonderful peoples are faithful followers of other religions.[1] Most of the time our questions are more philosophical. Who am I to say? These peoples are far removed. Most Hindus live in India. Most Buddhists live in Southeast Asia. Except for the lonely missionary in some far away land, rarely do we come head to head.

Now, however, things are different. Islam, for example, has brought some of the issues to the doorstep of Christendom.

## Chapter 5: "What About the Other Religions of the World?"

The photo at the head of the chapter (though not necessarily typical of Islam) was taken in London. Although the "Jesus only" question has already been addressed, in part (and will be addressed in even greater detail in a later chapter), for now, how does Christianity compare with other religions? What about the authority of the Bible? How do we agree, or disagree, on the big questions of life and death? For the sake of time and space, we focus on Islam.

If you want to make 9/11 worse than it already is, just keep on believing that Babylon is still in Iraq. It is not. It moved west. Throughout the Old Testament the nation Israel was supposed to destroy the Asherah poles, those pagan totems that dotted the landscape in times of idolatry. One day it occurred to me that if you cut those poles down, burn them, bury the ashes and then leave them in the ground long enough, *they turn to oil*. We simply have different pagan gods. It concerns me that the U.S.A. has an oily tail wagging an oily dog. Since most of the oil is in the hands of the Muslim world, we had better learn how to get along.

### The Five Pillars of Islam

I was recently asked for advice for a grant proposal involving Islam. My response went something like this: Those who hand out grants usually look for something that explores new and needed areas of interest for the broad spectrum. *Presently no one in your field is doing much about reconciliation with Muslims.* How can we hold to the uniqueness of our faith in Jesus Christ but still extend the hand of peace? We evangelical Christian types (like most Americans) usually lack humility and global perspective. We need to know the Qur'an and we need to make an honest attempt to understand the world from its perspective.

According to the Qur'an, Allah sent 124,000 prophets including Adam, Noah, Abraham, Moses and Jesus. Muslims believe that Muhammad was the last of these prophets and served as their seal. Beyond this, everyone should at least know the *Five Pillars of Islam,*

- Islam's understanding of truth consists of two fundamental affirmations (*Shahada*): "I bear witness that there is no God but Allah; and that Muhammad is his Prophet (or Apostle);"[2]
- To pray five times a day (*Salat*)—preceded by ritual washing and facing Mecca;
- To give alms to the poor (*Zakat*)—especially during festivals and the Sabbath (sunset on Thursday to sunset on Friday);
- To fast during the daylight hours of the month of Ramadan (*Sawm*).
- To make pilgrimage to Mecca at least once in one's lifetime (*Hajj*).

Some Islamists add an optional sixth, the holy war or *jihad*. Remember that much of Islam must endure the desert, and if you do not understand the desert you will never understand the Qur'an and its images of heaven as wonderfully green and replete with water (Surah 18:3, et al.). Furthermore, life in the desert is always a struggle. In fact, *jihad* is the Arabic word for striving. As you anticipate your grant proposal, I ask you to take all of this into consideration.

### An Encounter with a Muslim

Do you understand what others believe about God? That poses yet another challenge to the Christian faith today. Last year I was on a panel in Chicago with Christians and Muslims. Since the intent was to encourage interfaith dialogue I came looking for ways of affirming what is good in Islam—their faithfulness in prayer, their commitment to the poor, their level of fidelity in marriage, their sobriety. These virtues would challenge any Christian. So, when my Muslim friend said that the Qur'an does not teach violence I did not object, though I could have quoted Surah V, 33:

> The punishment of those who wage war against Allah and His apostle [Mohammad] and strive to make mischief in the land [a most interesting phrase in light of the war in Iraq] is only this, that they should be murdered or crucified or their hands and their feet should be cut off on opposite sides or they should be imprisoned, this shall be as a disgrace for them in this world, and in the hereafter they shall have a grievous chastisement.

In fact, I could have cited dozens of similar passages but I simply listened, UNTIL he asked this question: "Have you read the Qur'an lately?" Since I read the Qur'an through carefully every year I was about to respond when he added this, "Christians do not have a reliable or authoritative Scripture [like the Qur'an]. The Christian Bible has been changed so many times since the King James Version was written in 1611 that no two versions are alike" (he apparently believed that the KJV was our original text, and I must admit if that were true it would make some of my fundamentalist friends downright giddy). I said, "Sir, I must tell you that you have been misinformed. We do indeed have a reliable Scripture and since our Canon was established in the fourth century (which I might add predates the Qur'an by some hundreds of years) it has never been changed from the original texts."[3] I then asked, "Where did you hear such a thing?" His reply left me nearly speechless, "From Christian seminary professors and from the books they recommend." These books apparently insisted that the Bible was simply a book of collected sayings, and some fine poetry, but was certainly not believed to be the Word of God in any unique sense. My response was that your taking the word of those particular professors and books would be like my taking the word of Salman Rushdie (*Satanic Verses*).

You must know that I'm no fundamentalist (in fact I tend to make fundamentalists nervous), but may I say that when so-called Christian theologians give Islam reasons to reject the Christian faith and hold more firmly to what I believe to be a misguided (and dangerous) interpretation of the Old Testament (the Qur'an), I'm really scared (and more than a little bit angry). Let God (or Allah) arise!

**Can I Trust the Bible?**

How should I have responded to such a statement? What are the rules of engagement? My usual response is, "Be humble, but not too humble." If you struggle with your own view of the Bible as authoritative, let me tell you another story by way of illustration.

I once walked into a seminary faculty luncheon only to discover that several of my colleagues were laughing at the idea that one of our students believed that the book of Daniel was written in the sixth century B.C.(when it claims to have been written). Their argument was that since no one believes in predictive prophecy and Daniel speaks so specifically about events that obviously refer to the time of the Maccabean revolt (middle to late second century B.C.), it could not possibly have been written before 168 B.C.

As I sat down next to one of my closest friends I leaned over and asked, "Isn't Daniel in the Dead Sea Scrolls?" His muffled reply could still be heard by all, "You know it is. That's my Ph.D. dissertation." I then asked, "Can you carbon date those parts of the Dead Sea Scrolls that contain the eight or so references to Daniel?" He nodded with a bit of a smile, "Within a decade or two." I nudged him, "Well?" He actually blushed, "Probably around 250 B.C."

Another colleague immediately objected, "Well, that may be, but everyone knows that if you whispered a message in one ear on this side of the room, by the time it was transmitted to

## CHAPTER 5: "WHAT ABOUT THE OTHER RELIGIONS OF THE WORLD?"

the other side of the room, no one would recognize the original message."

God forgive me but I thought to myself, "Lord, you just delivered this dear man into my hands." I asked my friend just one or two more questions, "Have you compared the Dead Sea Scrolls with the next earliest manuscript we have of Daniel" (It happened to be 450 A.D.)? Since the focus of his dissertation had been the comparison of these two manuscripts after seven hundred years of transcribing, we all waited for his reply, "Not one iota was out of place." In other words, the scribes had taken such great care with transcribing what they believed to be the Word of God, not one letter was missing.

May I say to you now, in all honesty, I really do believe that the Bible is the Word of God and that the revelation that led to the writing of the Bible is totally reliable. Let me explain. I just admitted that I'm not a fundamentalist. I hasten to add, however, that there are plenty of Christian fundamentalists (or Muslim fundamentalists for that matter) who are smarter than I am. It's just that it is difficult for me to believe that revelation extends to the choice of the words on the page—"verbal plenary inspiration." It seems to me that God reveals the images behind the word (a right brain function), and then trusts the left sides of our brains to provide the articulation. That would account for the different styles of writing so evident throughout the Scriptures. Paul no more wrote the Book of Hebrews than I wrote "Twelfth Night" or "Romeo and Juliet."

Let me give you an example. If I were to draw a stick figure on a blackboard of a man running downhill (though I'm no artist) I could get consensus from any class as to what I had drawn—a man running downhill. Fundamentalism believes that the Holy Spirit revealed the words, "man running downhill," while I believe that the Holy Spirit revealed the image behind the word (a right-brain function) and trusted the left side of the brain to provide the articulation, guaranteeing that whatever words were necessary to describe the event accurately were included on the page. Now, does that mean that fundamentalists believe the Bible anymore than I do? I think not. I believe the Bible is the only absolute truth. In fact, when I'm not quoting the Bible, what I have to say is only approximate truth. If I did not believe that, I would have nothing to preach. My theology would probably be the latest book I had read. Furthermore, because I believe the Word of God to be trustworthy, I read it constantly.

For thirty-five years I've purchased a new Bible every year. On the first of January, I (and six to eight of my students) begin reading and marking four chapters a day of the New Testament, starting with Matthew. By early March I've finished the New Testament. Then, I begin reading and marking four chapters a day of the entire Bible, starting with Genesis, so that by the end of December I've completed the Old Testament once and the New Testament twice. At that time I give the Bible away and begin reading all over again on New Year's Day. I've given away nearly thirty-five Bibles over the years. It works for me, but I hasten to add that I am not necessarily recommending this for every Christian. What is freedom for one might be bondage for another. I am asking you to take the Word of God seriously and to know it well.

### Rules of Engagement

In any culture, when competing for the hearts of people, if Christians do what they do best (treating people with love and respect, while serving, praying and forgiving), and the world does what it does best (accumulating money, power and status), Christians should win every time. I meet people all the time who make three/four times what I make, and after thirty minutes they want to be me. You would love my life. Yet, I'm troubled as an American.

Francis Fitzgerald wrote, "Americans ignore history. . . . They believe in the future as if it were a religion; they believe that there is nothing they cannot accomplish, that solutions wait somewhere for all problems, like brides."[4] Manifest destiny is always putting on new dresses, and we Americans are getting deeper and deeper into trouble. Without humility and global perspective it will always be *we* and *they*.

> All good people agree,
> And all good people say,
> All nice people, like us, are We
> And everyone else is They.
> But if you cross over the sea,
> Instead of over the way,
> You may end by (think of it!)
> Looking on We as only a sort of They![5]

I might add, or, "Looking on They as only a sort of We."

Still there is a point at which we need to be able to respond to the honest inquiry. Just in the past week a Muslim friend reacted to my question about his need for revenge. I had just read an article sent to me from former students in the Indonesian province of Suwalesi.[6] I had taught there some years ago. Although that province is evenly divided between Muslims and Christians, three Christian girls had just been beheaded. The Muslim suspect told the judge, "We are not cold-blooded killers. . . . We just wanted revenge." He then apologized to the girls' parents as if they were not to take it personally. "Family and friends are honor-bound to take revenge." I wondered aloud, "What if revenge goes on and on, until eventually no one can remember the original offense. Revenge is taken against those taking revenge and then revenge against them in turn. The cycle never seems to end."

My Muslim friend simply said, "It's about war and that's what *jihad* is all about. I could show you dozens of statements about war in your own Bible." I said, "The Old Testament speaks about war, but the Qur'an is an interpretation of the Old Testament just as our New Testament is an interpretation of the Old Testament (or the Mishnah, the Talmud or even the Book of Mormon for that matter). You can never make a case for war (let alone revenge) from the mouth of Jesus. Jesus interprets the Old Testament in an entirely different way from Muhammad. Muhammad calls for war, "'those who disbelieve, strike off their heads'" (Surah VIII, 12-16); Jesus calls for peace, 'love your enemies and pray for those who persecute you' (Matt. 5:44). Can you help me understand that? It seems to me that we may both be wrong, but we cannot both be right. We disagree." He shrugged and walked away.

Leon Uris' *The Haj* describes a chilling conversation between the leader of a Muslim village overlooking a Jewish kibbutz across the road between Tel Aviv and Jerusalem (wars have been fought over this road) and a Jewish leader. The Muslim leader's name is Ibrahim (What else?) and the Jewish leader's name is Gideon (What else?). At one point in the story Ibrahim confesses that Gideon is his worst enemy, but his only friend. Then this exchange ensues, beginning with Ibrahim,

> "During the summer heat my people become frazzled. They worry about the autumn harvest. They are drained. They are pent up. They must explode. Nothing directs their frustration like Islam. Hatred is holy in this part of the world. It is also eternal. If they become inflamed, I am but a muktar. I cannot stand against a tide. You see, Gideon, that is why you are fooling yourselves. You do not know how to deal with us. For years, decades, we may seem to be at peace with you, but always in the back of our minds we keep up the hope of vengeance. No dispute is ever really settled in our world. The Jews give us a special reason to continue warring."
>
> "Do we deal with the Arabs by thinking like Arabs ourselves?" Gideon mused. . . .

## CHAPTER 5: "WHAT ABOUT THE OTHER RELIGIONS OF THE WORLD?"

> "Aha!" Ibrahim said. "That proves you are weak and that will be your downfall. You are crazy to extend us a mercy that you will never receive in return."
>
> "The Jews have asked for mercy a million times in a hundred lands. How can we now deny mercy to others who ask it from us?"
>
> "Because this is not a land of mercy. Magnanimity has no part in our world. You Jews have come in and destroyed a system of order we created out of the desert. Perhaps the bazaar looks disorganized to you, but it works for us. Perhaps Islam looks fanatical to you, but it provides us with the means to survive the harshness of this life and prepares us for a better life hereafter."[7]

Now, having established the contrast between Islam and the Christian/Jewish tradition, let me give you some basic principles as rules of engagement:

*First*, earning credibility and trust, or the right to be heard, requires patience and understanding. Try never to react without asking the question, "Why?" It is always important to understand the other person's point of view. It seems to me that, if following the tragedies of 9/11, had we paused just long enough to ask "why" rather than vowing revenge and preparing for war, we might have served the cause of peace and security far better. How can people possibly hate Americans that much? Is it simply a matter of jealousy or have we offended the rest of the world at some deeper level? Has our insatiable need for things driven the two-thirds world even deeper into poverty? Please don't write this off as liberal tripe. I'm a red-blooded American. Democracy seems to work in America. I'm even a capitalist, but it seems to me that democracy and capitalism ought to produce better products and services, not avarice and greed.

*Second*, attentive listening means being present and engaged.

Francis of Assisi was known to say, "Preach at all times and when necessary use words."[8] Sometimes we have to be silent to be heard. Many years ago I was sitting next to a woman on a long transcontinental flight. She was reading a current best-selling book, *Looking Out for Number One*. Since I had just assigned that book in a class I was teaching, I was curious as to her impression. "Oh, it is one of the best books I've ever read. The only way to get ahead is to look out for yourself, *first*. No one else really cares." She then told me that she was a buyer for a large department store in New York City. For some reason I asked, "Do people work for you?" With some pride she announced that thirty people were directly responsible to her. My next question was nearly the last thing I said for the rest of the flight, "Of the people who are responsible to you, tell me about the ones who subscribe to the philosophy of that book." Over the next several hours she told me about how difficult it was to turn her back on any of them. They were making her life miserable, and she was making their lives miserable. By the time we were ready to land, she had concluded that she no longer liked the philosophy of that book (she actually left it on the plane) and no longer wanted to be that kind of a person. I'm telling you the truth, all I did was ask the question and listen.

*Third*, sometimes prayer can lead to a timely and sometimes surprising word. I was sitting on an elevated train in Chicago with my back to the window facing rows of seats not three feet away. There was no one else in this particular car except for an elderly couple, seated directly in front of me. At the next stop two young women entered the train and took the seat just behind the couple. One of the women was smoking a cigarette. The elderly gentleman simply turned around and said that he was allergic to smoke, and since there was a no smoking sign on the window next to her would she mind extinguishing the cigarette. The woman reacted instantly. She blew smoke in the man's face and then, while cursing, slapped him on the back of his head dislodging a rather obvious toupee. When the woman saw the toupee she began laughing, snatched it off his head and began stomping it. At that point the train stopped at the next station. The elderly couple hurried off, pausing only long enough for the man's wife to grab the toupee on their way out.

So, there I was, not three feet from these two women. In a matter of seconds I had watched this abuse unfold in front of me, and if I said nothing I would explode. I remember praying, "God give me a word; I cannot sit and remain silent." At that moment the abusive woman looked at me, and I heard something come out of my mouth that absolutely astounded me. It felt almost out of body. "You have incredibly beautiful hair" (which she did; it was braided and beaded and seemed to cascade down her back like waterfalls). Instantly her entire countenance changed from a grimacing snarl to a radiant smile, at which point her companion poked her in the ribs saying, "See, see, see how good that makes you feel? Why were you so mean to that old man? Why didn't you say something nice to him so that he could feel good, too? You got an attitude, girl. You're my best friend and you embarrass me." At that the woman hung her head, obviously ashamed. Since we then arrived at my stop I nodded at the woman's friend, mouthed the words, "Thank you," and exited being utterly amazed. The woman's friend had said all the things that I had wanted to say, and more. There has to be a moral there somewhere.

*Fourth*, no one should ever think that you think he or she is stupid because he disagrees with you. I was a boy Ph.D. When I returned to the U.S. after completing that degree abroad, I honestly believed that I was the church's favorite son. This was during the middle '60's, and when I was assigned a church in the rural South I soon realized that the most segregated hour of the week was between 11:00 and 12:00 o'clock on Sunday morning. I decided to act. A local radio station was looking for public opinion and offered me a slot. I begged the people of that particular county to integrate their churches. When I walked out of the station they were waiting for me. They did not have on their gowns and hoods, but I knew who they were (half of them were members of my church). Before I could open my mouth they dragged me by the tie under an old oak tree and proceeded to beat the "mischief" out of me (to this day I still have lumps on the back of my head and scar tissue on the inside of my lip). I recall that my first reaction was utter confusion. How could they do this to me? I was their pastor. Then, sometime later I realized what I had done. *I had gone into a community with the answers before I knew what the questions were.* I probably had about half of that beating coming. Though my opinions on justice issues have never wavered, I'm now, I hope, a whole lot wiser. Even when I'm wrong, my wife has a way of disarming me with the occasional compliment. I then spend the rest of my life trying to live up to it.

*Fifth*, my sphere of influence relates to people I like. The more people I like, the greater my sphere of influence. When I find that I like people I begin to pay closer attention to the opportunities for ministry. Wonderful things are about to happen. Similarly, when I find that I do not like people, I'm in trouble. In the church mentioned above, someone was programmed every Sunday to stand and grumble the moment I "got off text" that they were not going to listen to that bull **** any longer. I cannot tell you how disconcerting that was for a young minister of the gospel.

Once while standing in the pulpit, just before I was to preach, I realized that I really disliked about half the people in the congregation. Suddenly, I simply excused myself, saying that I had something I needed to do. I would probably return. At that point I went back into my office, shut myself in the closet, sat on the floor with my head on my knees and prayed, "God I cannot do this anymore. I'm not going back out there if you don't give me a love for the people." I cannot adequately explain what happened next. Within moments I sensed God saying, "I give you the same love I will one day give you for your own children." Boom! My life was changed. I felt I did love the people, and when I returned to the pulpit, miraculously no one had left. They tell me that was the best sermon I ever preached. My ministry has been different ever since.

**Some Perspective on Islam**

Islam is perhaps the most fundamental challenge for Christians today. As a religion, Islam appeared fairly late (early seventh century). Let me give you just a bit of the detail. First of all, their sources:

Apart from the *Qur'an*, the second most important source of authority is the *Sunna*—meaning "trodden path." The *Sunna* consists of the words and actions of Muhammad as recorded in the traditions of Hadith. A third source of authority, the *Shari'a*—meaning "the path"—is drawn from the *Qur'an* and the *Sunna*. The *Shari'a* is the body of law for the Muslim community. This community is of critical importance. Muslims will generally help each other in a crisis. They take pride in a lack of discrimination in this community, and thus, are growing among peoples who have experienced discrimination— especially from Christians. This is, no doubt, the reason for the rapid growth of Islam among African-Americans in North America. In fact, over the past few years Muslims growth in the United States has been the highest in thirty years—43,000 in the first nine months following the attacks of 9/11/01.

I was in Israel just before the Gulf War of 1991. In November 1990, twenty-one Palestinians were killed on the Temple Mount. Although I do not get nervous easily, things were tense, and I decided to travel to northern Africa until things cooled off a bit. While traveling by bus in the Gaza Strip from Ashkelon to Rafah, just north of the Egyptian border, suddenly a couple of thousand Palestinians were blocking the road—four more Palestinians had been killed in the Strip that afternoon. The bus driver said, "Folks, this is the end of the line." Not thinking clearly, I stepped off the bus, hoping to catch another ride to the border, just a few kilometers farther south. As the bus made its turn back to the north, the taillights suddenly disappeared as the crowd closed in. I was feeling lonely. Suddenly an Israeli troop truck—sirens blaring—broke through the crowd. Seeing me, they quickly pulled me into the back of the truck and took me to a military compound nearby where I was given a bed and a telephone. The next morning I asked directions to the border. "Just down the road. During the daylight hours you will probably be safe hitching a ride, as long as the license plate on the car is yellow (Israeli) and not white (Palestinian)." On the road, a car with white plates immediately stopped to give me a lift. Since I did not wish to seem ungrateful, I climbed in. The driver immediately looked at me—twice—and pointed, "You're the man on the road last night." When I admitted the undeniable, he simply placed his thumb and index finger just centimeters apart, "You came this close. Here, have a banana." By the time we arrived at the border I had a sack full of groceries. As I was getting out, I had to ask, "Let me see if I've got this straight. Last night you wanted me dead, this morning you give me a lift and a sack full of groceries. Can you explain that for me?" He smiled and said, "You don't understand the Arab mentality. In mass, we had far rather hate our enemies than love our friends, but one on one we give you the shirts off our backs." Several years later, on a plane to Bahrain sitting next to a Muslim, I decided to test that maxim. When I told him this story his immediate response surprised me. "You are correct. In fact, when we make *Hajj*—our pilgrimage to Mecca—we have prayers to pray as we walk around the city on seven consecutive days. On one of those days, we must pray this prayer, 'Allah, protect me from the mischief of the crowd.'"

The man in the automobile was a *Sunni*. The man on the plane was a *Shi'ite*. Since most non-Muslims don't have a clue as to the difference, let me explain. During the Umayyad

Caliphate Dynasty (seventh/eighth centuries) the capital was moved from Baghdad to Damascus—where it remained for the next ninety years (661-750). During that time the *Sunnis* split—an argument over the succession to Muhammad—into *Sunnis* and *Shi'ites*. *Sunnis* still *comprised the large majority* and today are *predominant in most African countries, India, Pakistan and Indonesia.*[9] They *are led by community consensus—ijma'—* and accept the first four caliphs (or Umayyad Dynasty rulers) as the legitimate successors to Muhammad. The *Shi'ites*—or *Shi'a—tend to look more to a specific spiritual leader or imam who is viewed as God's representative on earth.* They consider Ali, Muhammad's son-in-law, to be the first imam. Unlike the *Sunnis, the Shi'ites have an institutionalized clergy who exercise great authority*—note the power of the Ayatollah Khomeini and the present leaders in Iran. Today the *Shi'ites are predominant in Iran, Iraq, Bahrain, and Azerbaijan.* Then, when the Abbasid Dynasty replaced the Umayyad Dynasty and the capital was moved back to Baghdad, the *Shi'ites* split again, this time into Zaidis and Ismailis. Since the differences are more political than religious, let me mention just one other group—the *Sufis*.

*Sufism—Sufi* means "mystic"—is a mystical movement that began during the same period (*c*. 750).[10] In contrast to the more fundamental branches of Islam where Allah is far removed, these Muslim ascetics sought direct personal contact with God. With the present-day rise of Islamic fundamentalism, however, these mystics are becoming more and more difficult to identify. Interestingly, so are most of the more mystical Christian traditions where peace is preached and passivism is a matter of practice.

### So How Do We Get Along?

It should be fairly obvious that no one wins the war against Islam. Christians have been battling with crusade vigor for well over a thousand years. Neither will Islam win the war against Christianity. Historically, when Christians are persecuted for being Christian, the nail is simply driven deeper. So how do we get along?

First, we determine to do what we do best according to Christian principle: we love and forgive, maybe *one Muslim at a time*.

Second, we feed the hungry, clothe the naked and visit the sick and imprisoned. May I remind you that the radical Hamas (Sunni) won the elections in the Palestinian Authority because they were the ones most effective at feeding the hungry and educating the children? The majority believed that the PLO was too busy stuffing its pockets with American money.

Third, we learn to get along with other Christians. The greatest threat to Islam is not American bombs. It is war among themselves.[11] The same could be said for Christianity. Let me illustrate.

I was recently in several of the Balkan countries: Croatia, Montenegro, Bosnia/Herzegovina, Slovenia and Serbia. Those who understand the Slavic peoples know that the conflicts there (especially during the "recent" war of 1991 to 1995) go back literally a thousand years. This was the epicenter of the fight between Christian (Eastern) Constantinople and Christian (Western) Rome that split the Slavic people into two groups—the Serbs (Eastern) and Croats (Western). Both speak a similar language and both are basically the same ethnically (albeit with some Turkish intermixing with the Serbs and some German intermixing with the Croats). Slobodan Milosevic's uncle was killed in WW II by the Utashe (the Croat Nazi collaborators under the leadership of the Bosnian Croat, Ante Pavedlic), hence, his hatred for the Croats was established because of the holocaust in his own family (nearly 600,000 Serbs were killed in WW II, largely by Nazi collaborators). So there are demonic strongholds of ethnic hatred in the Balkans! Furthermore, historically Bosnian Muslims were once Christians who followed a heretic named Bogomil and the so-called Bogomil heresy. Both Catholics and Orthodox slaughtered them like sheep; so, it is no surprise that they converted en masse to Islam when the Turks conquered the area in the early part of the sixteenth century. So, the recent war was not so much between Christians and Muslims (though Christian Serbs and Muslims eventually fought in Bosnia); it was between Christian Serbs and Christian Croats.

Like politicians slamming each other on the eve of an election, we tend to cancel each other out and undermine the people's confidence in the political (or religious) systems altogether. Both Christians and Muslims alike had best learn from the words of Thomas Paine, "If we don't learn to love each other, they will hang us one by one." We tend to be like two lawyers suing each other for malpractice, both win their case and both are disbarred.

Fourth, we learn to pray with authority. Jesus might well say, "This kind can come out only by prayer and fasting" (Mark 9:29). It is also good to remember that although both Christians and Muslims fight the demonic, we must never demonize each other. Although I, as a Christian, believe that it is faith in Jesus Christ alone that accesses the power of the Holy Spirit to overcome the sin in my life, that does not make the rest of the world my enemy.

Lord, teach me to pray and empower me to be more like Jesus. Like Paul with regard to his Jewish kinsmen in Romans 9-11, my only hope for winning my Muslim friends is to make them jealous. Does my life demonstrate more compassion, more joy and more power than any other? Could faith in Jesus Christ empower the Muslim to measure up, even to the Islamic law? I once led a Muslim in London to faith in Jesus Christ by simply helping him realize that the only way he could measure up to the Islamic law was to access the power of the Holy Spirit through repentance and faith in Jesus Christ. In other words, the only way he could become a true Muslim (he had struggled to be a faithful Muslim for years) was to become a Christian. There is something in me that believes that the only way to live up to any law, be it Christian, Muslim, Hindu or Buddhist is to access the power of the Holy Spirit. I sometimes say that true spirituality is not grunt and groan—it is repent and believe. I've found that *jihad* rules every aspect of Muslim existence. Our Muslim friends *strive* to be faithful to Allah and *strive* to obey the Muslim laws and *strive* to survive in a world that is never easy. So, how do we engage? First, we pray for ways of getting along. We really don't have to kill each other. Then, we make them jealous.

In the meantime, for those who are looking for hope among Muslims be encouraged by words from Wafa Sultan, an American-Syrian Muslim psychologist, "The Jews have come from the tragedy and forced the world to respect them, with their knowledge, not with their terror; with their work, not with their crying and yelling. We have not seen a single Jew blow himself up in a German restaurant. We have not seen a single Jew destroy a church. Only the Muslims defend their beliefs by burning down churches, killing people and destroying embassies. This path will not yield any results. The Muslims must ask themselves what they can do for humankind, before they demand that humankind respect them."[12] I might add that we Christians also must learn from anyone who opts for peace and has the courage to take the words of Jesus seriously,

> You have heard that it was said, "Eye for eye, and tooth for tooth." But I tell you, do not resist an evil person. If someone strikes you on the right cheek, turn to him the other also. And if someone wants to sue you and take your tunic, let him have your cloak as well. If someone forces you to go one mile, go with him two miles. Give to the one who asks you, and do not turn away from the one who wants to borrow from you (Matt. 5:38-42).

Need I say, that we who speak the name of Jesus Christ

do not always do this well? Many peoples of the world hold Christians in utter contempt? *Too many on whatever side believe that if they are right that makes the rest of the world their enemy?* Once again I believe that Jesus says it best,

> You have heard that it was said, "Love your neighbor and hate your enemy." But I tell you: Love your enemies and pray for those who persecute you, that you may be sons of your Father in heaven (Mt. 5:43-44).[13]

### The Rest of the Story

Earlier in this chapter I told the story of being delivered to the Egyptian border by a Muslim Palestinian. Let me tell you the rest of that story. Since I was arriving early in the morning, long before the border opened, I first of all spent nearly three hours chatting with the Israeli guards. We actually compared wallet photographs and talked about life in our various homes. I liked these people. Then, when the gates opened, I made my way through customs and passport control to the Egyptian side of the border. There I was looking for a bus to take me to Suez and then across to Cairo. The immediate reply from the Egyptians guards was, "No problem, five minutes."

Five hours later I was still waiting, during which time I chatted with the guards. We also actually compared wallet photographs and talked about life in our various homes (after looking at a picture of one of my daughters they offered me 100,000 camels as a suitable dowry). I liked these people, but still no bus.

At that point I began chatting with a Palestinian family, complete with three children and a mother-in-law. I had noticed a stretch taxi sitting by the road steaming from an overheated engine. I suggested to the couple that we might try hiring the taxi to take us to Cairo. I would pay half. They agreed and the taxi driver was delighted for the business. As we drove deeper and deeper into Egypt (stopping every thirty miles for water for the radiator) the radio blared and I got a splitting headache. Whenever the driver looked out his window I turned the radio down, but whenever I looked out my window, he turned the radio up. It was going to be a long afternoon and evening.

When we arrived in Suez, the canal was so packed with American battleships (this was the buildup just before the first Gulf War) it took two hours to get a ferry to take us across. When we finally arrived in Cairo, the driver could not find the hotel recommended by the Egyptian guards. It was now totally dark and my head was pounding, so I asked the Palestinians where they were staying, "In a hotel that caters to Palestinians in an older part of the city." I brightened and asked, "Can I stay there?" They were apparently surprised. "Of course, but do you want to?" I was desperate. "Sure, why not?" As we pulled up to the hotel I realized that the first seven floors comprised a textile factory. The hotel was housed in the seven floors above the factory. As we made our way through a dimly-lit cavernous marble corridor, there was a giant freight elevator at the end that actually opened horizontally like the jaws of a giant crocodile. Once in the lobby of the hotel, however, they did indeed have a room, but they would have to charge me seven dollars a day for room and breakfast, and the toilet was across the hall. I was ecstatic. They then proceeded to take me to the top floor of the hotel to a rather large room with shuttered balcony doors extending from ceiling to floor. When I opened them, I could not believe my good fortune. The pyramids were lit up before me in all of their splendor. I stayed there for seven glorious days.

Unfortunately, just a week later, I was making my way through the city and heard sirens coming from the huge square opposite the well-known Egyptian Museum. An American had been killed by what was believed to be an assassin's bullet. I then realized that it was probably time for me to head back to Israel. I took a bus the next afternoon. When we arrived at the Egyptian border and the guards saw me exit the bus, they blew a whistle, tumbled out of the post, took formation and snapped to attention. The rumor had circulated that I was the one killed in Cairo, and they were so happy to see me that they actually passed me down the line, hugging me and then kissing me on both cheeks. I was flattered.

Watching all of this with some interest was a tour bus driver from Nazareth. Since it was the Sabbath none of the Israeli buses were running. Since he was a Christian, his was the only bus at the border. I asked if he could take me north. He said that he could, but that he could not charge me. Since the bus was empty I could take the fold-down seat in the front where the guide normally sits. I said goodbye to all of the Egyptians, hugged and kissed once more, and headed out for the Israeli side of the border. As we approached the Israeli gate, the Israeli guards saw me sitting in the front of the bus, and so help me, blew a whistle, tumbled out of the post, took formation and snapped to attention. As one of the guards banged on the door, it opened and I was escorted off the bus. I was passed down the line while they hugged me and then kissed me on both cheeks. Again, I was flattered.

As I got back on the bus the driver looked at me and asked, "Sir, who *are* you?" I said, "I'm nobody." He said, "No sir, you somebody. I've seen 'em kissed on one side of the border, but never on both sides of the border. You got to be somebody." Right then I realized that the rest of the story was even better than the first of the story. Now I pray daily that soon, Egyptian and Israeli guards will be hugging and kissing each other. What about Palestinians and Jews? Muslims and Christians? Stop! Pray for the peace of Jerusalem, and Gaza, and Cairo, and Damascus, and Amman, and Beirut, and Tehran, and Baghdad, and Kabul, and Caracas, and Delhi and Jakarta, and on and on until Jesus returns and establishes his peace on earth, once and for all.

**End Notes**

[1] For those interested, an "Appendix" provides a brief synopsis of most of the other major religions of the world.

[2] Like the Hebrew *Yahweh*, Allah cannot be pluralized.

[3] It should be noted that the Qur'an also went through the process of establishing a canon of texts, which Muslims now believe to be authoritative. There is also a doctrine of "Abrogation" that is concerned with the modification of previous teaching contradicted by a new portion of teaching from Allah.

[4] Francis Fitzgerald, *Fire in the Lake*.

[5] Rudyard Kipling, "We and They."

[6] Indonesia (presently the world's fourth most populated country) has the world's largest Muslim population.

[7] Leon Uris, *The Haj*, pp. 60f.

[8] Interestingly, in the early thirteenth century Francis of Assisi joined the Fifth Crusade, not as a warrior but as a peacemaker. Friar Francis was not impressed by the Crusaders. Their brutality horrified him. They were entirely too fond of taunting and abusing their Muslim prisoners of war. See *Mysteries of the Middle Ages* by Thomas Cahill.

[9] It is interesting to note that Osama bin Laden and Al Quaida are Sunni whereas most Iraqis are Shi'te with a so-called Sunni insurgency.

[10] *Sufi* is from the word, *suf*, for "wool," what the early Muslim ascetics wore.

[11] It should be noted that the Sunni Hamas in the Palestinian Authority was in rare sympathy with the Shi'ite Hezbollah during the 2006 bombings in Lebanon.

[12] Dr. Sultan's life has been threatened for her March 2006 comments on the Arabic TV station Al-Jazeera. She said what few Muslims dare to say even in private.

[13] Cf. Luke 6:27, 35.

CHAPTER SIX

# "HOW CAN BAD THINGS HAPPEN TO GOOD PEOPLE?"
## (THE AGE-OLD QUESTION)

I get this question (or a variation of this question) in every course I teach. It's older than Job. The photo above is of a building in the center of Osijek, Croatia, still pocked with mortar and rifle fire surrounding a faded Communist star taken over ten years after a war that ended in 1995. During that war whole hospitals were emptied and everyone slaughtered. I've seen the mass graves outside Vukovar. I've also seen the mass graves outside Phnom Penh, Cambodia, called "the killing fields," where more than two million people were murdered on a ten-acre plot between 1975 and 1979, sometimes simply because they could read or wore glasses. There is a five-story Buddhist Temple in the middle of that field filled with nothing but human skulls.

I've also been to central Africa. What of the mass genocide in Rwanda? What of the holocaust? I've been to the concentration camps that still display the gas chambers and ovens as a reminder of how the innocent suffer. And that only scratches the surface of the twentieth century.

Pause for a moment to put a bit of the nineteenth century into perspective. Just over fifteen years after Wellington dispatched Napoleon at Waterloo, fifty million people died—mostly in India in 1831—during an epidemic of cholera. Another hundred thousand died in England from the spread of that same epidemic before medical research traced the cause to polluted drinking water. Over the next thirty years, another thirty-five million people were massacred during the T'ai P'ing Rebellion in China (that approaches nearly 300 a day), and this was after the Opium Wars (1839-1842) and before the Great Boxer Rebellion (1899-1901). Krakatoa erupted again in 1883, spreading a gloomy pall across the globe, followed by an influenza epidemic six years later that affected forty percent of the world's population—millions died.

Even in this century we think of Darfur. Then there are tsunamis and earthquakes and hurricanes, and, of course, HIV/AIDS, all devastating the innocent. Last week a young 12-year-old neighbor girl died as a result of a totally unpredictable accident in a horse barn. We had her mother over for supper last night, and she is struggling with the "Why? . . . Why do bad things happen to good people? She was such a sweet child, so bright and full of promise. Why? People tell me that God took her in his own good timing, and now she is an angel. That only makes me angry."

**A Question of Freedom**

Just let me be God for about thirty minutes and the problem of evil goes away. I would rip a hole in the heavens, stick my head down through it and shout folks into the Kingdom. There would be no sin in *my* creation. So, what's the problem? Why doesn't God just take my advice?

The answer to that question is fairly straightforward; you would have to give up your freedom. You and all of creation would dance at the end of my string, and (once again) your freedom is important to a God who gave us that freedom so that our response to grace might be genuine and heartfelt.

Another version of the problem of evil came by email just today. One of our brightest students received the doctor's sentence of death. If God does not intervene, she will die by way of pancreatic cancer. Her response? Not, "why me?" but rather, "why not me?" Jesus does not promise to deliver us from trouble. In fact, he guarantees it. He does, however, promise to deliver us from defeat. It is not a sin to be sick or to die (unless you are sick or dying because there is no one to pray for you). I promise to pray for this dear woman everyday until God heals her, one way or the other.

**The Broader Perspective**

I find that the answers to bad things happening to good people are first of all cosmic. Somehow God's good creation went awry. The theology of the Fall has already been discussed. Given enough rope, creation will hang itself from Haman's gallows.[1] Nevertheless, if God is such a good God and seemingly many of the promises of the Bible predict good things for the faithful, how can the faithful sometimes seem to suffer while the unfaithful seem to prosper? Is it all in ones perspective? Does God work with smoke and mirrors?

Let me make a confession. As much as I love the Word of God, I find some parts of the Old Testament especially troublesome. Take the book of Joshua, for example. Joshua "destroyed all who breathed, just as the LORD, the God of Israel, had commanded" (Jos. 10:40). How can a good God call upon Joshua and the children of Israel to cleanse the promised land of men, women and children? So, I ponder.

Perhaps those within the land had sinned away every ounce of good that was in them so that there was no longer any good left to respond to God (remember Sodom and Gomorrah). I know that God passes judgment on the "wicked." But kill all the women and children? History proved that those spared lived to teach the Israelites their pagan ways and soon led them into sin. But slaughter sheep and goats? I believe that if there were innocent among those killed that God drew them instantly into a paradise of love and beauty. But destroy all who breathed? It got so I could not read Joshua (or some of the other so-called history books, for that matter) without getting more and more confused. This seems to me like ethnic cleansing of the worst sort. In fact, you put all this into a contemporary setting and NATO bombers are zeroing in on the Ark of the Covenant. Then I had an experience.

### Not Yet Enough Light (NYEL)

Early one morning as I was reading I got an insight (I believe from on High). It went something like this. "Tuttle, you need to decide once and for all who I am." I said, "OK, God, here goes. From all that I read in the Bible, I believe that you are a God of love, mercy, justice, faithfulness and longsuffering." I then sensed God saying, "Not bad. From now on, whenever you read anything in my Word, or see anything in nature (like tsunamis, earthquakes, and hurricanes), or hear of anything in human nature (like mothers drowning babies or zealots flying airplanes into tall buildings), that seems out of character with a God who is loving, merciful, just, faithful, and longsuffering, you're going to have to realize, Old Son, that you do not yet have enough light, because regardless of what you see and experience, I really am a God of love, mercy, justice, faithfulness and longsuffering." Believe it or not, once I got that settled I could once again read Joshua (or any other part of the Bible for that matter). Nevertheless, those who inherit my used Bibles can still find these letters scribbled throughout the margins, NYEL.

## Disasters Created by Humans (The Devil Made Me Do It)

Many of us can remember the old Flip Wilson skits, where his character claims that the Devil made him do it. Although I assure you that the Devil can never coerce us into doing evil, there is some truth to this. We are in the midst of a war where battle lines are not drawn in desert sands, but in the heavens.

> For though we live in the world, we do not wage war as the world does. The weapons we fight with are not the weapons of the world. On the contrary, they have divine power to demolish strongholds. We demolish arguments and every pretension that sets itself up against the knowledge of God, and we take captive every thought to make it obedient to Christ (2 Cor. 10:3-5).

Much of the evil done to good people has the enemy of God at its core. The apostle Paul speaks of false apostles as "deceitful workmen, masquerading as apostles of Christ. And no wonder, for Satan himself masquerades as an angel of light" (2 Cor. 11:13-14). Imagine a young Muslim, when he is out of work and out of hope in a dry and dusty war-torn land being promised by the enemy (like the serpent with Adam and Eve) a garden paradise filled with wine, women, and song, and suicide is not so far-fetched, especially when martyrdom promises even greater rewards (Surah 3:15, 133, 136, 168-171).

So, what do we do? Are we helpless pawns (collateral damage) on some cosmic battlefield where those doing war are far beyond our control? Not according to Paul. We have available to us weapons with "divine power to demolish strongholds" (2 Cor. 10:4). So, when we speak of evil within the realm of human nature we can take the offensive. Jesus has taught us to pray and fast that we might overcome. His Spirit is at work within us, and that Spirit is greater than the spirit who is in the world.

OK, that gives us some hope for bad things of human origin. What about those quirks of nature that rain on the just and the unjust?

**Disasters of Nature (God is with Us)**

Three years ago I taught in Sri Lanka and visited many places that now no longer exist. Nearly every one of my students lost some family member to the tsunami that struck the day after Christmas, 2004. If prayer works, should I pray that storms go somewhere else to devastate some other unsuspecting peoples? Hardly. If the truth be known I'm getting older and wiser, and stupider and stupider. The only sense I can make of it all is that God never promises to deliver us from trouble. We, like the rest of the world, are just as vulnerable to mishap and destruction. God does, however, promise to deliver us from defeat. Can you find hope in these words?

> Therefore, since we have been justified through faith, we have peace with God through our Lord Jesus Christ, through whom we have gained access by faith into this grace in which we now stand. And we rejoice in the hope of the glory of God. Not only so, but we also rejoice in our sufferings, because we know that suffering produces perseverance; perseverance, character; and character, hope. And hope does not disappoint us, because God has poured out his love into our hearts by the Holy Spirit, whom he has given us (Rom. 5:1-5).

God apparently not only promises to deliver us from defeat, but also God promises to be with us in the midst of the fire. I love the story of Shadrach, Meshach and Abednego in the book of Daniel. When Nebuchadnezzar took an oath to throw them into the blazing furnace if they would not deny their God, they replied,

## CHAPTER 6: "HOW CAN BAD THINGS HAPPEN TO GOOD PEOPLE?"

> If we are thrown into the blazing furnace, the God we serve is able to save us from it, and he will rescue us from your hand, O king. But even if he does not, we want you to know, O king, that we will not serve your gods or worship the image of gold you have set up (Dan. 3:17-18).

With that the three men are thrown into the furnace, a furnace so hot that the heat consumes those delivering them to the fire. When the three men do not perish, Nebuchadnezzar leaps to his feet in amazement. "Weren't there three men that we tied up and threw into the fire? . . . Look! I see four men walking around in the fire, unbound and unharmed, and the fourth looks like the son of the gods" (Dan. 3:24-25).

Son of the gods, indeed. He was the Son of the living God, and his Spirit follows you into every furnace, whether it be earth, wind or fire. God can always save, but apparently sometimes chooses not to until we are face- to-face, on the other side. Speaking of the other side, Thomas Merton says, "The gate of heaven is everywhere." It is a question of dimension. Up and down went out with Copernicus. If we had eyes to see, heaven is all around us, just beyond the five-dimensional box of height, width, depth, time and motion. Ironically, heaven's gate is sometimes ground zero in New York City, or the Pentagon, or a field in rural Pennsylvania, or a train station in Madrid, or the London Underground, or an Embassy in Tanzania, or a horse barn, or a hospital, or a busy highway, but there is always that fourth man who stands with the faithful until we are "safe"—one way or the other—on the other side.

Last night rather than answering our neighbor's question, "Why?" I thought to ask her what (if anything) had the loss of her daughter taught her about God. I was ready to flinch since I knew she was angry. Imagine how impressed I was when she said, "God has been with me through it all, loving me, assuring me, giving me hope for a reunion when I cross to the other side."

I rarely quote poetry but there is a poem by James Russell Lowell that speaks to me time and again,

> Once to every man and nation,
> comes the moment to decide,
> In the strife of truth with falsehood,
> for the good or evil side;
> Some great cause, some great decision,
> offering each the bloom or blight,
> And the choice goes by forever,
> 'Twixt that darkness and that light.
>
> Then to side with truth is noble,
> when we share her wretched crust,
> Ere her cause bring fame and profit,
> and 'tis prosperous to be just;
> Then it is the brave man chooses
> While the coward stands aside,
> Till the multitude make virtue
> Of the faith they had denied.
>
> By the light of burning martyrs, Christ,
> Thy bleeding feet we track,
> Toiling up new Calv'ries ever
> With the cross that turns not back;
> New occasions teach new duties,
> ancient values test our youth;
> They must upward still and onward,
> who would keep abreast of truth.
>
> Though the cause of evil prosper,
> yet the truth alone is strong;
> Though her portion be the scaffold,

and upon the throne be wrong;
Yet that scaffold sways the future,
and behind the dim unknown,
Standeth God within the shadow,
keeping watch above His own.[2]

**Hope for a Better Day**

Why would Jesus teach us to pray, "Give us this day our daily bread"? Because the manna provided in the wilderness went putrid after more than one day. It could be gathered only one day at a time. It occurs to me that we do not have grace sufficient for tomorrow's troubles because tomorrow's troubles are not yet at our throats. Jesus says, "…do not worry about tomorrow, for tomorrow will worry about itself. Each day has enough trouble of its own" (Matt. 6:34). The point is that we do have a right to expect grace sufficient for the day.

Life is full of surprises, some good, some not so good. Someone has said that the Arts are forever creating new planets and not all of them are friendly. So, the challenges are never ending and totally unpredictable. Nonetheless, we press on because God is faithful.

Once again, be encouraged. "No temptation has seized you except what is common to man. And God is faithful; he will not let you be tempted beyond what you can bear. But when you are tempted, he will also provide a way out so that you can stand up under it" (1 Cor. 10:13).

The problem of evil? Why bad things happen to good people? Perhaps to teach the world how to endure the fire and sustain one's hope for a better day.

**End Notes**

[1] The gallows built by Haman, the enemy of the Jews, for Mordecai in the book of Esther. He was eventually hanged from his own gallows.

[2] "Words:" James Russell Lowell, in the *Boston Courier*, December 11, 1845.

CHAPTER SEVEN

# "WHAT ABOUT LIFE AFTER DEATH?"
## (HOW CAN I STOP GRIEVING?)

This chapter is obviously related to the last. Pain and suffering are often eager to question the existence of God and challenge the tenets of faith. Grief is not far behind. The sculpture pictured above is of Adam and Eve grieving over their slain son, Abel. How much worse when one child is murdered by the hand of another. How do you deal with that? I just returned from the funeral of the young girl mentioned in the previous chapter. I stated there that she died in a totally unpredictable accident. How do you account for all the things that had to come together for such a tragedy to take place? I had seen her riding happily across our mountain property many times.

The church was packed. The well-meaning pastor said words to the effect that this was all a part of God's plan. I cannot tell you what I was feeling inside. I wanted to scream, "NO!" This was not God's plan. God allows things to happen, but this was not God's plan. This was a tragic accident, and God was there grieving with the rest of us. God was sustaining the mother as she fulfilled a promise to sing at her daughter's funeral if the daughter should be the first to go. God was strengthening a father who was consumed with thoughts of what he possibly could have done to prevent such an accident. God was with a little sister who, when asked how she felt, was confused, "I don't know, Sis never died before." God was reassuring the middle school cross-country team, who would miss their star runner in a meet set for that afternoon. God was comforting grandparents and aunts and uncles and friends, who simply could not make sense of it all. Then, the words, "'I am the resurrection and the life. He who believes in me will live even though he dies; and whoever lives and believes in me will never die' Do you believe this" [John 11:25-26]? Yes, I said to myself, I believe that, but many of my friends don't.

How many times do I encounter honest doubt (sometimes looking like rage) in the face of tragic death? A movie from some years ago, "The Open Range," pictured two men standing over the shallow grave of a young man brutally murdered. One man asked the other, "Do you want to pray?" The other man looked him full in the face and with bloodshot eyes, shook his head, "Hell no! I'm not talking to the SOB who allowed something like this to happen!"

Most of us would not be so brazen but many of us, in like circumstances, could have had similar thoughts. In fact, not to have such thoughts could say more about us than they do about God. I shall never forget the words of an old stoic spoken to his wife when she thought she had lost her facial beauty to smallpox, "Wife, you were just too vain." Even worse, when grieving over the children she had lost to the same disease, "You loved them too much." Surely, there's a Word from on High to deliver us from such extremes.

> Even though I walk
> through the valley of the shadow of death,
> I will fear no evil,
> for you are with me;
> your rod and your staff,
> they comfort me (Ps. 23:4).

**Susanna's Baptism**

I walked into a hospital room to congratulate a young couple on the birth of their little girl, Susanna—their first child. I was instantly aware that something was terribly wrong. The couple was crying and the little baby lay dead on the mother's breast. Between the door and the bed I caught an image of taking that little baby, placing her in a basket on the River of Life and watching that basket drift slowly downstream. As I was describing this scene to the new mother and dad, suddenly I saw the basket flowing past the old man, Abraham, who stooped over, took her from the basket, held her to his breast and said these words, "I get to raise this one, you get to raise the next one." Then as the mother's tears flowed freely, I simply ran my finger along her cheek and baptized little Susanna with her mother's tears.

Once again, never mind the theology here. Susanna's baptism was not for her benefit, it was for the benefit of her mom and dad, and for me. I baptized the "next one" just two years later.

What do you make of these words from Jesus?

> Do not let your hearts be troubled. Trust in
> God; trust also in me. In my Father's house are

many rooms; if it were not so, I would have told
you. I am going there to prepare a place for you.
And if I go and prepare a place for you, I will come
back and take you to be with me that you also may
be where I am (John 14:1-3).

This text tells us that our eternal life is predicated on the
resurrection of Jesus, who goes to prepare a place for us.

**I Believe in the Resurrection**

Let me confess. I believe in the bodily resurrection of
Jesus. There is a bishop in my own denomination who believes
there's no such thing as a bodily resurrection, which he refers
to as "resuscitation." What? Who in the history of the church
has ever tried to make a case for resuscitation? Jesus was not
resuscitated like Lazarus or the boy of Nain.[1] Jesus came out
of the grave, not with his physical body, but with a glorified
body transformed from a physical body. I'll admit, although
I'm certain what went into the tomb (a crucified body), I'm not
so exact as to what came out of the tomb. But one thing I know
for sure, he left nothing behind. The man's body was glorified,
"the first fruits of those who have fallen asleep" (1 Cor. 15:20).
The stone had to be rolled away, not to let Jesus out, but to let
the rest of us in.

> But if it is preached that Christ has been
> raised from the dead, how can some of you say
> that there is no resurrection of the dead? If there is
> no resurrection of the dead, then not even Christ
> has been raised. And if Christ has not been raised,
> our preaching is useless and so is your faith. More
> than that, we are then found to be false witnesses
> about God, for we have testified about God that he
> raised Christ from the dead. . . . And if Christ has
> not been raised, your faith is futile; you are still in

your sins. Then those also who have fallen asleep in Christ are lost. If only for this life we have hope in Christ, we are to be pitied more than all men (1 Cor. 15 12-19).

Let me ask a rather pointed question. If you are having difficulty believing in the bodily resurrection of Jesus Christ, *who did what with the body*? I promise you the Romans did not remove it. They were the ones who sealed the tomb with the stone. The Jews would never take it. They were the ones clamoring for crucifixion. The disciples could not have taken it. Who builds and then surrenders their lives on what they know to be a hoax? All (but one) were martyred before the end of the century.[2]

Furthermore, if Christ has been raised, and indeed goes to prepare a place for us, what should our attitude be toward death? I've already admitted to being an old man. When you get to be my age, dying is no big deal. I pray that I can die with dignity and grace. My father wrote a book nearly every year of his retirement (fifteen or so). He always claimed he would do so until he died. I recall one day when he announced, while holding up an autobiography, "This is my last book!" I retorted, "So, what are you going to do now, die?" He instantly smiled and winked, "I might." He was dead within six months. The last words of that autobiography describe my father's difficulty in swallowing pills, "I ask Jesus to help me, and he does. One day soon, when I am about to die, I will ask Jesus to help me slip to the other side, and *he did.*"

Just after Christmas nearly two years ago my mother decided it was time for her to die. She was ninety-four. When her kidneys shut down the pain in her back made it impossible to sleep, so I crawled in bed with my mother, placed her head on my shoulder, put my arms around her and rubbed her back while praying ("God take away the pain, let her go to sleep, and take her home") and singing (she was the only person on earth who thought that I could sing) till morning. Around dawn she looked at me and said, "Robert, you've no idea how much you help me." Then a couple of hours later she said, "Robert, goodbye," and sank into a profound sleep. The next day I saw her on the undertaker's table. My sweet supple little mother was now hard as stone. Death had turned my mother into an "it." So, I put an "it" in the ground next to my father's "it" while they rejoiced together in heaven.

My little sister died from complications due to Alzheimer's some years ago. She was sweet to the end. She is now with Jesus. Do I miss her? Of course I do. I'm not a brick. Would I want her back? Only if you could talk *her* into it. She left this world with a mind that had deserted her years before, and exchanged it for a spirit that knows the very mind of God. Would you want to come back?

Thornton Wilder's *Our Town* makes the point. The stage is set with empty chairs representing graves. As the "dead" take the chairs, they begin talking among themselves. Emily describes her happiest day on earth—her twelfth birthday. When given the chance to return and relive that wonderful day, she jumps at the opportunity, but as the day progresses, she is increasingly disappointed. After bounding down the stairs announcing happily, "Hello, lucky people, your birthday girl is here," she begins to realize that her wonderful day might not have been as wonderful as she remembered. Mom was busy cooking, Dad was off to work and the children were out to play. Finally, at the end of the day she stands alone on that stage in despair, "Won't somebody please look at me?"

So, what about our attitude toward grieving the loss of loved ones and friends? Let me tell you a story.

### Where is Honey?

I have a Japanese-American friend who lives near Chicago. She introduced herself to me with these words, "My husband and I met in a Japanese interment camp during the war. He died ten years ago, and I grieve for him more now than I did then. In fact, I grieve for him more today than I did yesterday. It is affecting me more and more, and I do not want to go on living. I eat less. I sleep less. How can I stop grieving? All of my children are worried about me."

My first question was, "What's his name?"

"Honey, I always called him Honey."

My next question, "Where is Honey now?"

"He's in an urn in a Buddhist shrine next to my bed."

Then I asked, "No, where is Honey *now*?"

"OK, he's in heaven."

"So what's he doing?"

"He's playing golf. He always wanted to play golf in heaven."

I said, "You're grieving is getting in the way of his backswing. He would want you to get on with your life so he can get on with a decent round of golf."

Somehow my friend understood that. The next day she admitted to the best night's sleep in years.

It was then time for the next question. "What's up with the Buddhist shrine?"

"Oh, that belonged to my mother. She was a Buddhist but Honey and I are United Methodists. I keep it to honor her memory and as a place for Honey."

"What did Honey want done with his ashes?"

"He wanted me to scatter them on a beach in Hawaii."

"So why didn't you?"

"I miss him too much."

"I want you to do me a favor. I want you to take those ashes to Hawaii and fulfill Honey's wish."

"Oh, I can't do that. I've just returned from Hawaii. I can't go back for at least two years."

I repeated, "I want you to do me a favor. I want you to allow me to come to your home, to dismantle the Buddhist shrine (your mother will never miss it), and then to take Honey's ashes to your daughter's house for safe keeping until you can go back to Hawaii and fulfill Honey's request. For God's sake, let this dear man get on with his game of golf. You must be one giant handicap. Will you allow me to do that?"

She began laughing. "Oh yes. That would be wonderful."

The next day it was done and we still correspond. What's more, the church has now been able to gather around her for the kind of support that is sustaining her.

**"Gonna Lay My Isaac Down"**

Last year I preached in a large predominately African American church. I was struck by a special number sung by the choir, "Gonna Lay My Isaac Down." Suddenly it occurred to me, that's it. That's what the leap of faith is all about. Let me ask you a question. What's the most important thing in *your* life, right now? What do you think about before you go to sleep at night? What do you dream about? What's the most basic common denominator that supplies the ruling force for your life? That's your god. For my Japanese friend, it was grieving Honey. Stanley Jones said, "What has your attention has you." Furthermore, if you are worshiping a god that is less than God, you are worshiping a god that makes horrible demands but gives precious little in return. On the other hand, if you are worshiping the God that is God, you are worshiping a God that makes horrible demands but gives back, pressed down, shaken together, running over.

Can you identify your "Isaac"? Those of you who know the Genesis story of Abraham and his son Isaac know that Abraham's love for Isaac was supplanting his love for God. Let me explain.

Jesus says, "Anyone who loves his father or mother more than me is not worthy of me; anyone who loves his son or daughter more than me is not worthy of me; and anyone who does not take his cross and follow me is not worthy of me. Whoever finds his life will lose it, and whoever loses his life for my sake will find it" (Matt. 10:37-39). Let me illustrate.

In that little church on the southside of Chicago I put the word out that I would marry anybody for free (saving them the $5 for a civil ceremony), if they would spend two hours with me in counseling before the wedding, invite both sets of parents (they did not have to attend, but they had to be informed), show me a receipt for a room at some hotel (so they did not spend their wedding night in the back seat of a car) and pack a bag (so the bride's trousseau was not a change of underwear in a paper sack). You would think that I would get no takers. Think again. For the last year I was there I had on average 2 to 3 weddings a month.

During the counseling session I always asked, "What's the most important thing in your life. Inevitably the groom said the bride and the bride said the groom, while I said, "NO!" He or she will make a wonderful husband or wife, but he or she makes a lousy god. I sometimes asked the groom, "You want to be her god? He normally shook his head and I would add, "Let me tell you why. The moment she finds her security first of all in you and you do something that doesn't include her, it's a threat to her, and she clings and she nags. That's the way we treat our gods that aren't God. I would then ask the bride the same question. The only way to love your spouse the way God intended is to let God be God and to let spouse be spouse. Loving your spouse out of the reservoir of your own love never measures up to time and experience. Loving your spouse out of the reservoir of God's love measures up to time and eternity.

Gonna lay my Isaac down simply means to let God be God so we can love the rest of the world as God intended. I shall never forget the last Sunday I preached in that church. As I looked out from the pulpit nearly a fourth of the people in the congregation were couples that I had married.

Honey was a great husband but a lousy God. When my friend finally put that back into perspective, she was able to get on with her life and looks forward to a glorious reunion.

### So, What about Life after Death?

I'm always a bit puzzled by those who honestly believe that this life is all there is, that we are no more than a generation of leaves. Many of my own close friends have no hope or expectation beyond the grave. So, what do I say to them?

I'm sometimes drawn to the image of a chick still in its shell. As the chick matures and its beak hardens and its shell grows thin and begins to crack as the baby chick instinctively struggles against itself, I can imagine the chick thinking to itself, "Don't break shell. You are the only existence I've ever known. I'm afraid of losing your nurture and protection. I don't want to die." Then, unaware of its mother's warmth coaxing it out of its shell, it nearly despairs until the shell breaks and releases it into a whole new life of wonder and amazement.

Are my friends like that chick? I would probably never tell them as much; but still, I wonder.

One thing I know for certain. If there is a God and there is no life after death, then God is an unimaginable monster because there is absolutely no justice in *this* world. The only way for *this* life to make any sense whatsoever is for things to sort themselves out in the next. Surely that's why Jesus, in Luke 16, speaks of the incredibly selfish rich man (now dead) after he had consistently denied comfort to the poor man Lazarus, "Son, remember that in your lifetime you received your good things, while Lazarus received bad things, but now he is comforted here and you are in agony" (v. 25). There may be no justice in this life, but there will be a ton of it in the next. Although the logic of that argument may not seem conclusive, that alone is reason enough for me to believe. The apostle Paul would concur.

> I consider that our present sufferings are not worth comparing with the glory that will be revealed in us. The creation waits in eager expectation for

the sons of God to be revealed. For the creation was subjected to frustration, not by its own choice, but by the will of the one who subjected it, in hope that the creation itself will be liberated from its bondage to decay and brought into the glorious freedom of the children of God (Rom. 8:18-21).

Pilgrim, that's not just idle rhetoric, that's a promise and that's where I'm headed. Is there anything I can say or do to take you with me?

An ancient Jewish sage has written a word for all of us, "Though we speak much, we cannot reach the end; let the last word be: 'God is all in all.'"[3]

Several weeks ago I found a phrase written over the pulpit of a former synagogue—now a thriving Christian community—in Osijek, Croatia.

*Slava Bogu* [Praise God] and *Khristos voskres!* [Christ is risen!]

He has risen indeed, *for you!*

**End Notes**

[1] John 11:1ff. and Luke 7:11ff.

[2] John was the only apostle not known to have been martyred, perhaps a particular dispensation for taking Mary, the mother of Jesus, into his home (John 19:27).

[3] Ben Sirach 43:28.

CHAPTER EIGHT

# "MUST I BELONG TO A CHURCH TO BE A CHRISTIAN?"
## (WHY DO I NEED GOD OR OTHERS?)

The question, "Must I belong to a church to be a Christian?" can be preempted by another question, "'Why do I even need God?' Perhaps Karl Marx was right when he wrote, 'Religion is simply the opiate of the people.'" I admit, many peoples of the world, even if they do believe in God, usually don't live like it. They live their lives as if God really doesn't exist—until there's a crisis.

**We Need Each Other**

If you read straight through the Bible, two sins come at you time and again—oppressing the poor and being self-reliant. You really don't want to do either of those things. We've already addressed the results of the former (and will do so again). Now it's time to address the latter. Theologian Paul Tillich was right; sin begins the moment we attempt to become autonomous as if we could live apart from God, "the very ground of our being." *If utter reliance upon God is our greatest virtue, then complete reliance upon self is our greatest sin.* Yet isn't self-reliance the American way? Don't we applaud those who have supposedly pulled themselves up by their own bootstraps? That is not possible. Everything we do relates to God or it relates to nothing.

Self-reliance implies that I can do life on my own. Not true. Margaret Mead says we know that civilization was in place at least from the date of the earliest discovered human fossil with a healed broken femur. Obviously, the only way to survive a broken femur is for someone else to feed you.

Richard Leakey's book, *The People of the Lake*, makes a similar point. After digging around the old dry lakebeds in the southern part of Ethiopia, he surmised that between 1.2 and 1.5 million years ago four strains of humankind were evolving simultaneously. The theory had been that the strains to survive to evolve into modern humankind were the macho strains, the ones that went around smiting themselves upon the breast—the "survival of the fittest." Interestingly, Leaky discovered that those were the first to become extinct. Why? *They were loners and they got picked off.* The only strain that survived to evolve into modern humankind was *homo sapien*. Why? *Homo sapien was the only strain that dared to become community.* John Wesley commented when confronted with the dangers of mystic solitude, "We know no religion but social religion; we know no gospel but social gospel." We really do need each other. Furthermore, we really do need God.

### We Need God!

Few people knew this better than the biblical King David. Note the words from "David's Song of Praise" recorded in 2 Samuel 22,

> He reached down from on high and took hold of me;
> he drew me out of deep waters.
> He rescued me from my powerful enemy,
> from my foes, who were too strong for me.
> They confronted me in the day of my disaster,
> but the LORD was my support.
> He brought me out into a spacious place;
> he rescued me because he delighted in me (vv. 17-20).

OK, so far so good, but explain now how less than two chapters later, this same David calls for his commander, Joab, to "enroll the fighting men, so that I may know how many there are" (2 Sam. 24:2). Even an unrighteous commander like Joab knew the foolishness of such a census (in effect relying upon one's army for protection and not totally upon God), "Why does my lord the king want to do such a thing?" Later David would repent (perhaps the better part of his genius), "I have sinned greatly in what I have done. Now, O LORD, I beg you, take away the guilt of your servant. I have done a very foolish thing" (v. 10). Still, such attempts at self-reliance cost the Israelites 70,000 lives to a plague (v. 15).

A few chapters later (2 Kings 19:23-24), when Jerusalem was under siege by the Assyrians, the Assyrian king, Sennacherib, boasted,

> I have ascended the heights of the mountain,
> the utmost heights of Lebanon.
> I have cut down its tallest cedars,
> the choicest of its pines.
> I have dug wells in foreign lands
> and drunk the water there.
> With the soles of my feet
> I have dried up all the streams of Egypt.

The prophet Isaiah was quick to respond, "Against whom

## CHAPTER 8: "MUST I BELONG TO A CHURCH TO BE A CHRISTIAN?"

have you raised your voice and lifted your eyes in pride? Against the Holy One of Israel!" When Sennacherib boasted that if the gods of all the other cities had not been able to save, the God of Jerusalem would not be able to save, but once again Isaiah was quick to respond. "You speak of the gods of those other cities, you speak of the no-gods [literally little pellets of dung]. You speak of the God of this city you speak of the I AM God. Do not mess with the I AM God." That afternoon an angel of the Lord went and took out 185,000 of them and sent the rest of them back to Nineveh where they belonged (2 Kings 19:35). To this day you can walk through the Jewish Quarter of the Old City and see the very wall where Isaiah stood and made this pronouncement. We are utterly helpless without the God who is God.

Jesus says that "I am the vine; you are the branches. If a man remains in me and I in him, he will bear much fruit; *apart from me you can do nothing*" (John 15:5, emphasis mine). Self-reliant indeed. Still, I recall that as a young minister I thought that I could do it all. God was on call. I didn't need the church. The church needed me. I was their pastor. I really was in control, until. . .

### Somebody Is about to Shoot Me

I've already mentioned that my first church was on the southside of Chicago. This was back in the early '60's. I was twenty-two years old, but please don't do the math. My father reckoned that as a result of my ministry there I got twenty years experience in just over two. It was like living at warp speed. My wife calls many of these experiences my "Rev Stories." I'll tell you just one.

I remember driving up to the little church that sat directly on the street. The building had no locks, so I had no key. The moment we tried to lock the doors they were broken by would-be robbers, so we simply left them open. Still, as a young pastor I had a Messianic complex a mile wide. I honestly believed that the southside of Chicago was still a problem area because I had not yet arrived.

Apart from Sunday mornings, I remember making up excuses to preach, especially on special occasions. I invented a Thanksgiving Eve Service. Imagine my joy when the little church was packed. One of the members was crippled by arthritis. He was also a victim of alcohol. His wife brought him in a wheelchair. I shall never forget that when the invitation was given, the man suddenly stood and ran to the front of the church. He not only had an encounter with the living God, but he also was healed on the spot, utterly joyful. Over the next weeks and months we spent a great deal of time together. He was sober and pain free, and a testament to what God was doing in the Church. He was not only a member of my church, but he also became my friend.

Then, the 2 a.m. phone call, "Rev, come quick, there's a man over here about to shoot me." Never mind the logic of calling me rather than the police, I said, "No, he's not. Hold everything, I'll be there in ten minutes. I put my little Nash Rambler on two wheels around every corner and was there in five. As I approached the house every light was on (both floors). I went charging into the room where a crowd had gathered. There was a man holding a .44 on my friend. I said with what I thought to be the voice of authority while pointing at him, "You're not going to shoot my member!" He said, "Yes, I am, and what's more, I'm starting with you." As he turned, he shoved the gun up under my nose (it had a bore as big as a cannon). Then, as he laid the hammer back, I threw up all over him. Right then I had an epiphany: Just because you have the truth there is no guarantee the world will listen. That kind of experience is a guaranteed cure for the Messianic complex. As the man with the gun ran cursing to the bathroom to clean up, I prayed, "Thank God!" and called the police (which is what we should have done in the first place).

### Is Your God too Big, or too Small?

If honest doubt asks, "Do I really need God?" many of my friends ask, "OK, I'm cool with being reliant upon God for the big stuff, but what about the little stuff? Is it really necessary to bother God about parking spaces?" In a recent book on the history of evangelism, I had a chapter entitled, "A Transcendent/Immanent God." An understanding of *one* God who is both *transcendent* (who exists beyond the created universe and thus is not limited by it) and *immanent* (whose existence extends into all the parts of the created universe) is important. Belief in such a God seems to have little or no precedent in the ancient world. In the story of Abraham the concept of a God who—to state it simply—was both *without and within* was not just important; it was crucial to Abraham's understanding of his calling as a father of nations.

I'm convinced that God is big enough for the big jobs but small enough for the little ones, and delights when we make our requests known, be they for world peace, the health of an ailing friend, strength to overcome a haunting problem or even a convenient parking space to ease the frustration of a busy day.

### So, We Need Each Other and We Need God, but What about the Church?

I live in two communities, one in North Carolina and the other in Florida. My neighbors in Florida for the most part have no Christian memory. Many have not been to church in thirty years, even for weddings and funerals. How many times have I heard (especially during hunting season), "I can worship God in the woods better than I can worship God in a building. Besides, I hang out at the church on occasion, especially at Christmas and Easter. Must I belong to a church to be a Christian?"

I sometimes ask, "Why did you marry your spouse? Why don't you simply cohabitate?" With near offense they reply,

"We need the commitment." My next question, "Why would it be any different with the church?" If you live in the inner city and you're under twenty-five, you join a gang. Why? Because that's the only way to stay alive. To survive on the streets of any major city, you've got to have someone to watch your back. Now that's what church is really all about—having someone who knows you by name to watch your back by being there when you need him or her and by praying for you every day, by name.

We have already implied that Christians in the West tend to emphasize the individual, whereas the rest of the world understands community. Faith is not only an individual affair, it is a community affair. Watch what can happen when people come together in worship.

Last year I preached in a city in the Midwest. After returning home I received this email forwarded to me from the pastor. Although I've removed the names, I still run the risk of sounding self-serving, but I share it with you because it says a lot about the ministry of the Church.

*Dear Pastor,*

*You asked me to e-mail my story to you, so here it is from the beginning. I have been an insulin dependent diabetic since 1974—the only one in my family ever to get it. It has caused severe eye and kidney damage.*

*In August of '04, I was hospitalized for 1 week because my kidneys were shutting down. I was given more meds and discharged with high uric acid levels, which continued to erode the surfaces of all of the bones in my joints. In October of '04, I was re-hospitalized for three weeks and discharged in complete kidney failure. I required dialysis three times per week. My uric acid level was over 140 (high normal is seven). I could not stand without support and walking or transferring from the wheelchair without assistance was impossible. I was in constant pain and could not move any part of my body without tears running down my face. Sleep was almost impossible and never lasted more than an hour without being awakened by searing, burning pain.*

*I went home against medical advice. The doctors wanted me to be placed in a skilled nursing care facility. By the grace of God, another doctor made rounds in the dialysis center on my first outpatient visit. He told me that I had full body gout; [he] wondered why it was never treated and how could I tolerate the pain. I assured him that I wasn't tolerating it successfully. He put me on a new protocol. In three days, my uric acid level was significantly lower but the damage to my joints was untreatable. The only thing he could do was to give me pain meds. I had to live with the pain, which had diminished slightly. I remained on dialysis until late December of '04, when I regained enough kidney function to be temporarily taken off it. Eventually I was able to stand and walk independently but with persistent pain until I attended the healing service at church.*

*Pastor, during our earlier encounters, I felt acceptance and fellowship from you—a willingness to trust you. I believed that we would have a meaningful, personal relationship. It seemed that our understanding of God and His Son's teachings were remarkably similar. I hoped that I had finally found a church where I could be accepted—even welcomed as a member. I was excited to hear and discover more about the church.*

*Then, during our recent Festival of Faith weekend, I was surprised that the guest speaker would be lecturing on God's healing grace. I had been considering a pilgrimage to a cave in New Mexico where The Blessed Virgin is said to have recently appeared. Hundreds of miraculous cures have been reported to occur there. So the topic of healing caught my attention.*

*When the speaker started to talk, I was skeptical. I had not put God's healing grace and evangelistic preaching in the same category. Then he mentioned Oral Roberts, and I started looking for the exits, but my wife came in and sat next to me. I was trapped, so I decided to challenge and criticize everything he said. There was not going to be a "plastic Jesus" on my dashboard! I'm a big fan of St. Thomas, the doubting Apostle.*

*God bless the speaker. His sincerity and integrity were inspiring. I found myself captivated. His fervor and faith were unchallengeable. At times he said things that I had been telling my terminally ill clients for years. How could I challenge him?*

*After Communion, I went to the railing, knelt on the floor next to my wife and raised my hand. Then I began to have second thoughts. My knees were in severe pain, and I found myself looking for a polite way to tell my wife why I had gotten up and left. I didn't want to talk to the speaker or be anointed with oil out of fear that I would be disappointed again. I just wanted to find something to lean on to help me get up and leave. But, before I was able to escape, the speaker knelt in front of me.*

*When he cradled my head in his arm, I tried to tell him to let me get up. Instead, I started sobbing. I couldn't stop myself. Through all this, he helped me ask for help with my daughter's fiancé who had been estranged from us for months and for help with my kidneys. With God's grace and the speaker's example of his unflinching faith, I accepted the anointing and asked God for help. Then I returned to the pew with my loving wife. We sat there holding hands; letting tears stream down our faces as we prayed. I didn't notice anything unusual then or when we left church.*

*On the way to the car, my wife asked me to slow down. I stopped and looked at her in disbelief. I was pain free for the first time in over a year. I couldn't believe it. Then I remembered that I had no trouble getting up off the floor after the speaker had anointed me. I have been pain free ever since that moment.*

*Two weeks later, our future son-in-law spontaneously apologized for his outburst of anger. The next day, I went to my specialist. When we reviewed my blood work, there was a forty percent improvement in my kidney function over the last month. Things have remained stable since then.*

*I cannot effectively communicate my thanks to both of you. Please forward this to the speaker. Tell him I'm a "cohabitator" in*

## CHAPTER 8: "MUST I BELONG TO A CHURCH TO BE A CHRISTIAN?"

*the process of becoming a member of the Church.*

*God bless and keep you both in His hands. I will always be grateful to you.*

I wrote an immediate reply,
*Dear Brother,*

*God bless your heart. How do I thank you enough for your wonderful testimony? I like you; I like your wife; I like your future son-in-law; I even like your email address and that pastor of yours. Thanks for bringing your disease before the body of Christ and for getting "hitched" to the Church. That kind of commitment really is important. You and that fellowship of believers are the better for it. I'm asking God to raise up friends to gather around you, to pray that God will bring to completion the healing work already begun in you. Do keep in touch. Our paths will cross. In the meantime please believe that I remain, your real friend.*
*Bob.*
*Hos. 6:3.*

Need I remind you that this kind of miracle rarely happens in a deer stand or during a lonely walk through the woods. Like the paralytic in Mark 2, at some point the man had to be brought into the presence of Jesus.

### Want to Know Why I Joined a Church in Alaska?

Apart from the theological issues at work in the story of my friend on the southside of Chicago and the healing of this dear man here, how can the church gather around the lonely, the bereaved, the sick and the dying, so that Christian community is the gift that keeps on giving—right to the end?

Some months ago I was on a short flight to Atlanta. Seated next to me was a young man, probably in his mid-twenties. We said nothing to each other. I was tired so I spent the entire time in the air going over the sermon text for an evening message.

When we landed I stood to open the overhead bin and offered to hand him his bag. As I was reaching for the bag I heard a voice behind me say, "Would you like to know why I joined a church in Alaska?" Thinking he was speaking to someone else I simply turned around and handed him his bag, without comment. At this point, looking directly at me, he repeated the question, "Would you like to know why I joined a church in Alaska?" Somewhat puzzled I said, "Sure" (After all, we were exiting the plane so how long could this take?). For those of you who do not know the airport in Atlanta, the trip to the baggage claim takes nearly as long as some flights, so this story tumbled out over the next 20 minutes.

"A year ago I flew to Alaska to visit a friend for ten days. The day before I was to return he took me to church, a large contemporary-type building with a huge auditorium. I was resistant, as church had never been particularly meaningful to me. I was always too busy and, quite frankly, had never seen the point since most of my church friends did not live appreciably different than my non-church friends. My mother worried about my lack of interest.

"As I took my seat next to the aisle I noticed an attractive middle-aged woman directly in front of me. She was not only attractive, she was dressed to the nines. There was an empty seat next to hers. As the service began I noticed out of the corner of my eye a young man almost creeping down the aisle. He had that homeless look—unshaven, unkempt and unsure of himself. When the woman noticed him she stepped into the aisle, gave him an embrace, and directed him to the seat next to hers. For the entire service I watched her guiding this young man through the various aspects of worship. Then, as the preacher gave the invitation at the end of a tolerable sermon on the Good Samaritan, she leaned over and asked if he would like to go forward. He nodded, and I was surprised to see that she went with him. As they returned she gave him another embrace before they sat down and began to talk. I leaned over to my friend and said, "I guess she's really grateful that her son found God." My friend said, "I don't think that's her son." As they exited the room I had to know so I managed to stop her just before she left the building. 'Excuse me, ma'am. I could not help noticing you with that young man. Did you know him?' She smiled, 'Never saw him before in my life.' Immediately I pulled out my cell phone and placed a call to my mother here in Atlanta. 'Mother, I'm not coming home just yet. I'm about to join a church. I've just found a group of people that practices what they preach.' That church has changed my life. I followed that young man as he was accepted by a group of interested 'seekers,' including myself. Six months later we joined the church together."

Would you be interested in the kind of a church that knew you well enough to guide you to a group of like-minded pilgrims who understand you well enough to watch your back? Fortunately, this is not an isolated incident. There are thousands of churches with thousands of programs that understand the principle and would welcome you home. Let me mention just two local church programs that you might find helpful.

**The Alpha Course**

Several years ago my wife and I went to Cambridge, England, where I was a visiting scholar at the University for nearly six months. We attended King's College Chapel for worship most Sundays. The sermons were a hodgepodge of visiting preachers who rarely measured up to the wonderful choir. One Sunday, however, we heard a sermon that truly impressed me. Although there could not have been more than a couple dozen in attendance, this man preached the whole gospel. Afterward I greeted him asking, "Just who are you?" He told me his name was Sandy Millar, and he was the rector of Holy Trinity Brompton in the West End of London, and that we should visit them sometime. A few weeks later we were in London, so I dropped in for an evening service. It was packed and I was seemingly twice as old as the next youngest person in the congregation. I was impressed. A man named Nicky Gumbel preached and described a program originated by that church called the Alpha Course. I began reading. Now I'm convinced that although God never does just one thing, this is one of the things that God is doing in the Church today.

If you are interested in understanding the basic tenets of Christianity taught within a group-type experience, this is for you. The material is solid and communicates well at every level.[1]

### Emmaus Walk

I've just said that God never does just one thing. Another thing that God has been doing for several years is a program taken from the Roman Catholic Cursillo Movement. Twenty-five years ago I was asked to attend one of these long weekend retreats with the intent of taking the decidedly Catholic theology and adapting it to a more Wesleyan approach more compatible with Protestants. At that time I wrote a series of outlines for what are called the "Clergy Talks." I even wrote a book, *Sanctity without Starch,* to put flesh on those bones.[2] As I travel the world I rarely meet a group of Christians who have not benefited from these "Walks." If you are interested in the kind of experience that can get you in touch with what Christian fellowship should be all about, you can contact the Upper Room in Nashville, Tenn.[3]

### If Community Is the Key, Why Can't Christians Seem to Get Along?

So what do movements like the Alpha Course and the Emmaus Walk have to do with overcoming doubt? They help to understand Christianity at its best. They then provide community and the follow-up contacts that can guide and sustain you. They are designed to help honest seekers understand the work of the Holy Spirit. They get people in touch with their spiritual gifts. Being in the Church is not belonging to an organization, but an organism. It's not membership in a club but participation in a lively body. So, why can't Christians seem to get along?

Philippians 4:2-3 should break your heart. Paul writes, "I plead with Euodia and I plead with Syntyche to agree with each other in the Lord. Yes, and I ask you, loyal yokefellow, help these women who have contended at my side in the cause of the gospel, along with Clement and the rest of my fellow workers, whose names are in the book of life." Apparently two of the saints are having difficulty getting along. It happens. So, what's the problem?

The answer to that question had already been described in some earlier verses,

> If you have any encouragement from being united with Christ, if any comfort from his love, if any fellowship with the Spirit, if any tenderness and compassion, then make my joy complete by being like-minded, having the same love, being one in spirit and purpose. Do nothing out of selfish ambition or vain conceit, but in humility consider others better than yourselves. Each of you should seek not only to your own interests, but also to the interests of others (Phil. 2:1-4).

Reinhold Neibur once wrote, "In society the whole is less than the sum of its parts." That's because society tends to look after its own interests first. On the other hand, in the Church, the whole is (or should be) greater than the sum of her parts. That's because Jesus is the head of the Church, and if you had to reduce the words of Jesus to one sentence, it would have to be this (what I call *the first principle of Christianity*), ". . . whoever loses his life for me and for the gospel will save it" (Mk. 8:3, 6), because the only way to be great is to be a servant, and the only way to be first is to be last. For Jesus that principle was a constant theme. Unfortunately there are days and weeks when I forget the principle, when I don't want to be last. Worry about me. Pray for me.

I've forgotten who first said, "There is no limit to what you can accomplish if you don't care who gets the credit," but that is the mind of Christ. The old adage, "When the team wins, we all eat well," really is true.

I received a letter recently from a friend who wrote that "God is preparing me for something really BIG." I could not help but wonder, what is BIG? How does one give up one's life for Jesus, really BIG? How does one be last, really BIG? How does one be a servant, really BIG? I wonder if my friend wants to be like St. Francis of Assisi or Mother Teresa. Now that's BIG! Read Ephesians 4:2-6,

> Be completely humble and gentle; be patient, bearing with one another in love. Make every effort to keep the unity of the Spirit through the bond of peace. There is one body and one Spirit—just as you were called to one hope when you were called—one Lord, one faith, one baptism; one God and Father of all, who is over all and through all and in all.

### The Rest of the Story

As in a previous chapter there is a "rest of the story." This one relates to my friend on the southside of Chicago. Although he had been saved and healed and managed to survive an irate gunman, his enthusiasm began to wane. He and his wife began skipping church. I was told that his wife led him back to the bottle. Before his conversion she had been the wife of "a cripple and a drunk," and that's the way people related to her. She had their sympathy. After her husband's conversion, her friends began to relate to her differently. She was no longer the recipient of sympathy and received no special quarter. This confused her. So, one evening she enticed her husband to join her in just one drink, and then they both stayed drunk for more than a week. I was devastated. I recall visiting them. The house was ankle deep in cans and bottles and they were both passed out on the living room floor. I had a thought—nice guy that I am—I'll recruit a few friends and we'll clean the place up. They will love us for it.

We did it. I rounded up a few of the hardy faithful and we managed to get them both into bed while we washed, scrubbed and polished for several hours. They were still asleep when we left a note, "Because we love you."

That coming Sunday was Pentecost Sunday, and I had just written the finest sermon of my short career. As I prepared for church, I had a thought. Since I knew they would be grateful for the way we had cleaned up their house, why not drop by and invite them personally to come and hear this wonderful sermon. When the wife opened the door, I've never been so cursed and berated. She let me know in no uncertain terms that I was never again to come to their house, for any reason, whatsoever.

So, what had I done wrong? My condescending, self-righteous attitude had not only embarrassed them, it had shamed them also. No amount of apology could reach them. They were lost to me and to the church, and I was to blame. God forgive me. Pray that I learned that lesson well.

**End Notes**

[1] The Website for The Alpha Course is <alphacourse.org>.

[2] Robert Tuttle, Jr., *Sanctity without Starch*, Bristol House, 1992.

[3] The Website for The Emmaus Walk is <emmauswalk.net> or <upperroom.org/emmaus/>.

CHAPTER NINE

# "WHAT ABOUT FAITH AND DOUBT AND THE ISSUES OF POLITICS?"

(IS JESUS A REPUBLICAN OR A DEMOCRAT?)

At some point most of my friends (including my wife) advised me to omit this chapter, but then many of their questions relating to faith and doubt involve political issues. They are frustrated by some of the so-called faith-based initiatives and some of the apparent hypocrisy associated with them. The ridiculous slogan pictured at the head of the chapter captures some of that frustration.

Yesterday a well-known "evangelical" Christian was interviewed on National Public Radio. He was informing the audience about what we evangelicals believe on every issue from Abortion to Zionism. Since I do not like for others to speak in my behalf, as if all Christians (or evangelicals for that matter) believe as he believes, I must speak my own mind (in part) as a protest for many an honest doubter who has been turned off to Jesus by his so-called friends.

Without addressing specific issues so much as principle, what about the so-called Christian vote?" While George Hunter's book, *Christian, Evangelical, and . . . Democrat,* heads off in one direction (as a Democrat), I want to explore the broader ground as a way of addressing the issues of faith and doubt.[1]

Many of my friends would swear that Jesus is a Republican. In fact, during the Reagan Administration Republicans declared that they were *the* party of God. Others claim he's a Democrat. Since I am embarrassed (and/or encouraged) by something on nearly every platform, I'm not so sure. I frequently ask my students (whether Republican, Democrat or Independent) to vote Jesus (not their money-belts) on every issue. I've already mentioned a recent trip to Central Europe. The better part of a month was in Croatia. There (as in places like Iraq and Afghanistan), politics cost lives. One thing I've discovered, when the Church gets caught identifying with the oppressor, she loses face. Unfortunately history is replete with examples.

## To Identify with the Oppressor

From Kublai Khan to Mahatma Gandhi to Mao Tse Tung, when the Christian Church forgot the mind of Jesus, honest doubt turned to disappointment, resentment and grief, not to faith. When the Mongol, Kublai Khan, the "Christian Protector," died in 1294, the Church had failed him miserably. The Papacy was in disarray, and the requested missionaries (through Marco Polo) never arrived. *This marked a significant turning point toward Islam in Asia.* Ilkhan Ghazan, the Mongol ruler of Persia, converted to Islam the following year. He quickly destroyed all churches, synagogues and Buddhist temples. With Islam as the state religion, Nestorian Christians, Zoroastrians, Jews and Buddhists were massacred. All of the Mongol hordes were soon to follow as in the footsteps of Muhammad.

Gandhi's rejection by Christians in South Africa took him to the place where he could still follow Jesus, but not Christianity.

China, between 1911 (the "Last Emperor") and 1949 (when China fell to Communism), was open to Christianity. The wives of both Dr. Sun Yet Sen and General Chiang Kai-shek were Christians (and sisters). Unfortunately the Church, in spite of some well-meaning and courageous missionaries, became associated with the oppressors, while Mao Tse Tung and the Communists identified with the oppressed, and the Communists won the day in a matter of months.

I should also add that over the past thirty years as a seminary professor, whenever I found seminary students losing faith, it was almost always connected with some political issue. Having said that, may I confess to you that the Church's attitude toward political issues has been the greatest challenge to my own faith.

I mentioned in an earlier chapter that I had a difficult time loving some of the people in the church I was serving in the rural South. I recall being embarrassed by their attitudes toward people of color. My life was threatened on any number of occasions. I had so many crosses burned on my lawn that I stopped filling in the hole where they were planted. Let me tell you a sad story.

One of the members of that church boasted that if he ever caught me on his property, "I was his meat." Then his barn burned down. Being a "loving pastor" I went through the community collecting money to help pay for a new barn. When I drove out to his house to give him the money, I knocked on the screen door (the inside door was open). When he came to the door and saw me, he stepped back, kicked the door open. Before I could peep, he grabbed me by the tie (those were the days of big wide ties with large knots) and began swinging me around the barnyard on the end of my tie while beating me on the top of the head and screaming, "Why don't you hit me back? Why don't you hit me back?" All I could say was, "Jesus won't let me," but I'm not sure I was even capable of hitting him back. I had one hand in my pocket around the wad of money I had intended to give him but, like the monkey with his hand in the jar, I could not pull it out. My other hand was around the tie to keep him from choking me to death (the big knot was now about the size of a pea). Finally he tired and let me go, but as I was walking to my car he ran up behind me and kicked me in the seat of the pants. I remember saying, "Jesus, no man ought to take that off anybody. I'm going to get him one little one. I won't hurt him bad." I turned and looked him full in the face with blood in my eyes. He could tell I wasn't afraid. Then, just before I reacted, I heard that inner voice, "If you are going to preach the gospel, you best try and live it. This man is one of your sheep." I then simply raised my hand for him to stop, "No more!" went to my car and drove off.

His wife tells me he did not take his clothes off for days. I had him. He thought I was special because I did not hit him back. Then, several days later as I was walking out of the one local store with groceries in my arms, I saw him sitting behind the wheel of his truck while an attendant filled it with gasoline (this was before the days of self-service). I remember walking over, reaching my arm through the window, placing my finger against his nose and saying, "Buford, you better pray to God I never wipe out on Jesus, because if I do, I'm coming, and you're number one." You know what Buford did? He drove home, climbed into bed, and slept like a baby. I let him right off the hook. If I could have just kept my hands off him, I had him. He already knew I wasn't afraid of him, but I had to go and touch him and let him right off the hook . . . and I've worried about it ever since.

That experience did as much to challenge my faith (in God as well as in myself) as anything I've experienced. Believe it or not, it was a political issue. He believed one way and I believed another.

### To Identify with the Oppressed

On the other hand, my faith has been strengthened when the Church has identified with the oppressed. Then even people with doubt seem to listen. We've already mentioned the two big sins in the Bible—oppressing the poor and being self-reliant. Let's return to the former. Forgive the cliché, but I cannot tell you just how important it is to "walk the talk." Balance between personal and social is crucial. Need I remind you that the opposite of personal is not social, but impersonal, and the opposite of social is not personal, but antisocial?

To politicize sometimes means to demonize. We cannot see the other person's point of view, even amongst our brothers and sisters. Some evangelical Christians in Croatia tend to look down their noses at the Catholic majority (ninety percent), but fail to appreciate the strong Catholic view of the Church as the body of Christ. Far worse, we've just come through an off-year election. The campaign ads were so vitriolic it is a wonder that anyone voted at all. I said earlier that it is always counterproductive if others think we think they're stupid simply because they disagree with us. So we paint ourselves into corners. The newspapers quote the U.S. President, "Our fate hangs in the balance, along with much of the rest of the world. If we lose the war in Iraq, every other issue may be moot. The war the terrorists have declared against us is at stake. We have to do this one right, or the rest might not matter." This reminds me of a quotation from Mark Twain, "Those who do not read the newspapers are uninformed, those who do are misinformed."

I've already implied that I believe that no war with terrorism is ever won on the ground. If radical Islam is really the problem (as many would have us believe), then get out of the face of Islam and watch religion turn to ideology. People usually do not blow themselves up over ideologies. Look at the so-called "domino theory" in Latin America not sixty years ago. I remember the slogan, "If we do not stop Communism in Central America, all of Latin America will fall within ten years." It did not happen. Little Cuba is the only hold out. When any ideology overextends itself, it tends to wane. Forget the newspapers; read the history books. Viet Nam is now a tourist mecca—for Viet Nam War veterans.

**Pray for the Democrats**

"Pray for the Democrats" was the headlines in a recent online Christian publication after the Republicans had lost their majority in both the House and the Senate. These words followed,

> Our enemies [supposedly terrorists] are in full, triumphant cry, scenting weakness and the defeat of their enemies. Our allies are dismayed. Now most of the fate of the United States—indeed of the world—has been handed to the Democrats . . . .
>
> And the defeated Republicans? What will they do? Get even? Obstruct at every turn? Or work with their American enemies against the enemies of all Americas?
>
> Pray, Americans. Pray. Pray for the Democrats. Pray for the Republicans. Pray for our allies. Pray even—as the Bible instructs us—for our enemies. Pray for our incredible young men and women on the front lines.
>
> Above all, pray for our leaders. Since most of them are now the Democrats, pray for the Democrats especially. Pray for the newly minority Republicans. Pray mightily for our President, our one and only Commander-in-Chief.
>
> Worldwide peril and danger are increasing tremendously. Our future is being decided. We

must humbly, urgently, persistently petition
our God for the wisdom and help we need.²

OK, I'm confused. Do these words help or hinder the cause of Christ? Though the author of these words and I have virtually nothing in common, ideologically, she is still a good friend. I admire her tremendously. Yet while I agree with and applaud her plea for prayer (who wouldn't), her words here seem to miss the mark. The word "enemies" appears five times, and I'm not always sure whether it refers to the terrorists or the Democrats. What would Jesus say about all of this? As Christians, it keeps coming back to him.

**What Would Jesus Do?**
Although I'm not particularly fond of bracelets, the WWJD one seems to make the most sense to me. Here's a question, "What is the spiritual value of people engaging in community programs of justice and reconciliation without any clear understanding of the theological and historical truths that underpin their motivations? Jesus is the reason, not only for the season, but for all that we do. I pray for the end of injustice and the reconciliation of all peoples, but what can I do to motivate myself and others to try and make a difference?

Years ago, much to my dismay, I realized that no matter how good the program, if you are not properly motivated it will never work. Then I also discovered that no matter how bad the program, if you are properly motivated, you will find a way to make it work.

So, where does proper motivation come from? That brings us back to the issues of doubt and faith. God, whose side are you on, anyhow? What must I do to enlist your support? Instantly I sense the nudge, "What does the Bible say?" If God is our God and we are God's people, how can we be assured of God's protection and grace? Surely we begin by letting God be God. We trust God to be faithful to all of those wonderful promises.

The Old Testament is full of "ifs" and "thens."

> The Lord will establish you as his holy people, as he promised you on oath, *if* [italics mine] you keep the commands of the LORD your God and walk in his ways. *Then* [italics mine] all the peoples on earth will see that you are called by the name of the LORD, and they will fear you. The LORD will grant you abundant prosperity—in the fruit of your womb, the young of your livestock and the crops of your ground—in the land he swore to your forefathers to give you (Deut. 28:9-11).

Whereas the Old Testament speaks mainly of obedience to the law, the New Testament speaks mainly of justification by faith.

> It was not through law that Abraham and his offspring received the promise that he would be heir of the world, but through the righteousness that comes by faith. For if those who live by law are heirs, faith has no value and the promise is worthless, because law brings wrath. And where there is no law there is no transgression.
>
> Therefore, the promise comes by faith, so that it may be by grace and may be guaranteed to all Abraham's offspring—not only to those who are of the law but also to those who are of the faith of Abraham....
>
> ... to whom God will credit righteousness—for us who believe in him who raised Jesus our

Lord from the dead. He was delivered over to death for our sins and was raised to life for our justification (Rom. 4:13-16, 24-25).

That brings us back to Jesus.

**Was Jesus Political?**
Was Jesus political? You bet, just not yet. His political realm would not be realized until his return. Many of us should tremble at the thought. He came the first time as a servant. The next time plan on seeing him in power where justice will "roll on like a river" and "righteousness like a never-failing stream" (Amos 5:24). In the meantime, does the Bible address political issues? You bet. We've mentioned the poor but now include widows and children. Not moving your boundary markers and not gleaning the corners of your fields were all political issues. Taxes, weights and measures, even private ownership are all discussed at great length.

Evangelical Christians, by and large, believe that you cannot legislate morality. That should be left to the Church. Oh? Were civil rights not moral issues? Leave that to the Church and we are still a segregated nation. OK, what about the other side of the coin. Is abortion a moral issue? There are lots of people that wish the Church would leave that one alone. We evangelicals have turned abortion into a litmus test for politicians nationwide. Don't get me wrong, I'm against abortion–on–demand as if the life of the fetus did not really matter, but some knee-jerk reactions take away the rights of the mother altogether.

OK, here's a real challenge for faith. What about war? What would Jesus do on that one? If you are looking for a problem text, quote one verse and run immediately out of steam, "Do not suppose that I have come to bring peace to the earth. I did not come to bring peace, but a sword" (Matt. 10:34). You've seen the context for this already. "Anyone who loves his father or mother more than me is not worthy of me.... Whoever finds his life will lose it, and whoever loses his life for my sake will find it" (Matt. 10:37, 39). To my knowledge, never in the history of the Church has anyone ever interpreted that as if Jesus were making a case for war. Rather, Jesus says that if you follow me, the sword will come to you in all kinds of persecutions. The roads to Rome were lined with thousands of Christian crosses. On the eve of the Crucifixion, within the shadow of his own cross, Jesus gathers his disciples in an upper room to give them final instructions. Those instructions conclude with these words, "I have told you these things, so that in me you may have peace. In this world you will have trouble. But take heart! I have overcome the world" (John 16:33).

Not only has Jesus overcome the world, but he also expects us to overcome the world, not by bombs and bullets, but by loving our enemies and doing good to those who hate us and mistreat us (Luke 6:27f.). Does that mean that Christians can turn their backs on the oppressed of the world? Hardly. There is another kind of war that can be fought on a different plane.

### The War on Poverty

I don't give a fig whether you vote Republican or Democrat. Jesus and I are probably socialists. I do care, however, how we conduct our lives. The Church can no more solve the world's problems than the U.S. government, UNLESS we change our way of thinking, living and spending. On the issue of poverty, for example, how can we teach our people to enter into the struggle with integrity without also calling them to cease their endless pursuit of wealth? How can we build our economy on gas-guzzling automobiles and expect the rest of the world to understand our occasional handouts as affecting any kind of significant change?

Some of you remember Lyndon Johnson's "War on Poverty." Since that war lacked global perspective, I realized then the deep challenges proposed by such a noble program.

It was fairly obvious to me that if we were not willing to speak against excessive wealth, we had no platform to meet the poor as sisters and brothers, even in our own country.

When at least two-thirds of the world can never hope to achieve any real level of financial security, how do we avoid seeing our positions of wealth as the ideal? Even worse, won't we then measure our success on how effective we are in bringing people up to our impossible standards? Most of us now realize that the world will never have the kind of resources for everyone to share our Western standard of living. In order for the West to live as it lives, the rest of the world must do without. There is only so much planet earth can produce.

Then, what of the deeper call to live compassionately? Until we are willing to suffer with people (the true meaning of compassion) we, by default, will decide to break fellowship with those who have no ability to sustain themselves above the poverty level. How do we celebrate and remain thankful to God when the struggles persist among the poor of the world? Shouldn't it bother us that in some instances rock stars and country and western singers have more political clout (and are having more success in addressing the needs of the poor in the world) than the Church? Forgive me for saying it, but it seems to me that many of my evangelical friends appear paralyzed. We simply want the problem to go away.

Let's think for a moment about this same issue through the eyes of the global poor. If the poor of the world perceive that the Church's vision is to end poverty, how can they enter into such an impossible dream? Little wonder Jesus said, "The poor you will always have with you. . . ." (Mk. 14:7) If, on the other hand, the poor of the world see that our vision is to care, perhaps through loving, intimate relationships, then we stand with them against the injustices that cause poverty, and they can see themselves as entering the struggle as a part of the solution, not just a part of the problem.

Most of the peoples on planet earth honestly do not feel as if they have much invested in this present world. The problems are simply too big and they are simply too small. I have Hindu friends among the "untouchables" in India who have no hope whatsoever of ever improving their lot in this present world. Their only hope is for the next reincarnation. We have already spoken about the Muslim desert and the lure of a heavenly paradise. How's that for giving new meaning to "pie in the sky when you die." Don't we realize that most of the world lives on less than a dollar a day, yet we complain when immigrants flock to our borders to do the jobs that most of us don't want anymore.

So, how does a government become compassionate? We write to our representatives and ask them, "Please, stop doing the self-serving kinds of things that have a way of surfacing in the ads of your political opponents during the next election campaign." We talk about the needs of the oppressed and the poor in such a way that it is obvious that there are people out there *with votes* who care about such issues. Talk about humility and global perspective. Shouldn't we be afraid of our level of opulence? Most of you would not think me wealthy, but I have more than ninety percent of the peoples of the world. Sure, I'm afraid. I know full well that the only way to take it with me is to give it away. You'll never see a hearse with a U-haul trailer behind it. The best the pharaohs could do was to preserve their bodies so that they now look and feel like leather. God in heaven, please forgive me if I have hoarded or robbed You of the things that You intended for someone else.

### The Next Time you Vote . . .

The next time you vote take this verse into the polling booth with you, ". . . Jesus said, 'Simon son of John, do you truly love me?' He answered, 'Yes, Lord, you know that I love you.' Jesus said, 'Take care of my sheep'" (John 21:16).

**End Notes**

[1] George Hunter III, *Christian, Evangelical, and . . . Democrat*, Abingdon Press, 2006.

[2] This was posted November 11, 2006 on this website: gerrycharlottephelps.com.

CHAPTER TEN

# "How Can I Know the Will of God?"
## (The future)

Many an honest doubter stumbles over the angst of an uncertain future. I've sometimes gotten this question, "You tell me that God has more invested in my life than I do, then why doesn't God just appear and tell me plainly what to do next? How about a little handwriting on the wall?"

First of all that handwriting business—from the biblical perspective—relates more to warning than to promise.[1] Second, isn't life far more interesting if we leave the future for God to know and for us to discover in bits and pieces?

### Faith beyond Sight and Trust beyond Clarity

I once worked for Mother Teresa in Calcutta—just for three weeks. Although I actually never met this remarkable woman (she was apparently too busy to take time for making casual acquaintance), I felt her presence everywhere. One morning a priest came into the Home for the Dying and told me an interesting story. He had just spoken with the Reverend Mother at the Sisters of Charity Mother House (just three short blocks away), and she asked, "How can I pray for you?" His reply was heartfelt, "How can I know the will of God? I desperately need clarity for the future!" She smiled and shook her head. "You don't need clarity, you need trust." His response was immediate, "But *you* have clarity." She smiled again, "I've never had clarity. My life is from day to day." After I read her diary following her death I better understood what she meant. She lived with persistent uncertainty until the day she died.

Since that time I have been refining my own understanding of trust as it relates to faith. *Shouldn't trust get me beyond the need for clarity just as faith gets me beyond the need for sight?* Second Corinthians 4:18 reminds us, ". . . what is unseen is eternal." Let me confess something to you. I used to tell students that if I could ask God one question it would be, "What next?" I now realize that that's the wrong question. I need to ask God for trust (and an anointing), and then the "what next" takes care of itself.

If God were suddenly to appear within the senses (as if God were seated before you as I could be seated before you) it would not take faith to believe that God exists. That would remove the need for faith, in effect forcing us to believe (remember, if you cannot say no, your yes is meaningless). Similarly, clarity removes the need for trust. John Wesley, on the day of his "evangelical conversion," was consumed with doubt and thoughts of what it meant to trust God.[2] Just before he felt his "heart strangely warmed" at a meeting on Aldersgate Street, he was worshiping in St. Paul's Cathedral. Most Wesley scholars believe that the words of the anthem sung in the Cathedral that day were taken from Psalm 130 and frequently repeat the words, "Trust in the Lord." Wesley tells us in his *Journal* that these words had profound influence. Once the issue of trust was settled, faith was soon to follow.

So, if trust creates enduring faith for the honest doubter, how do we get to trust? Like Pascal, let me challenge you with an honest wager. Dare to trust God, and the Spirit of God promises to bear witness with your spirit that you are a child of God (Rom. 8:16). Little wonder that Wesley preached more on that text than any other. Know that *Christianity is self-authenticating*. If we are willing to risk believing (committing all that we know of ourselves to all that we know of God as the ultimate leap of faith), the Spirit of God guarantees an inner witness that sets our minds at ease. Let me illustrate out of my own experience.

### God If There Is a God . . .

I came to faith in Jesus Christ as a senior undergraduate at Duke University. I was twenty-one years old. I had gone to church all of my life but had rarely paid much attention to matters of faith. I was a harmless "Joe College," hopelessly preppy. Oh, I was never an atheist. It never occurred to me not to believe in God. I simply had not put much thought into God one way or the other. Then someone asked me a question at a party while I was visiting a friend at Wheaton College outside Chicago, "How long have you been a Christian?" I was puzzled, "That's a hell of a question. I'm an American for God's sake. My father is a minister. I was born a Christian."

Had she challenged that comment she would have met all of my resistance. Rather, she simply said, "Really? That's interesting," and walked away. Once again the age-old adage, "You put the pressure on by taking the pressure off," carried the day.

After returning to North Carolina, for the next two weeks I walked the streets of Durham wondering if there was something I needed to do to become a Christian. I asked my father. He sent me a Bible. I began to read it for the first time. Then, late one night I prayed this prayer: "God, if there is a God [and I wasn't real sure], Christ, if there is a Christ [and I was even less sure of that], I give my whole life to you. Even if you do not exist, from this moment on, I'm going to live as if you do." Now, that may not sound like much, but God called that prayer *faith,* and my life was changed forever. In a moment the Spirit of God bore witness with my spirit that I had been put right with God. Within days my world went from black and white to technicolor. I wanted to eat grass because it was my favorite color. I fell in love with the universe and everything in it. Then came the question, what do I do now?

Suddenly I was bored with the prospect of spending the rest of my life chasing dollars and climbing ladders. There had to be more to life than that. My lucrative career would have to be put on hold, but in the meantime, what do I do?

**All of Life Is Fraught with Uncertainty**

I have a student who was a physicist in the aerospace industry. She wrote to me recently regarding some questions I had about natural law.

> Discoveries in quantum mechanics tell us that there is uncertainty in the basic laws of physics. The Heisenberg uncertainty principle states that one cannot know the exact values, even in theory, for certain pairs of observable variables, such as the position and momentum of an electron orbiting around the nucleus of an atom. In measuring one attribute, the other is perturbed. That means God has woven uncertainty into the fabric of the universe. The universe is still governed by a set of natural laws that God made, but those laws include stochastic [I love that word] processes. Everything is not completely deterministic.[3]

Now there's a thought for those of us who like little

packages that are manageable and light enough to carry. As I contemplated my next move, I felt that I was in need of more faith if I was to embrace my own uncertain future. As a student, sometimes in the middle of class, a thought would consume me—if there is no God, you are a fool—and I would panic. One morning, after struggling through most of the night, I picked up the Bible given to me by my father and turned to the concordance, looking for faith. Hebrews 11 seemed to have lots, so I began flipping pages. Finally I found these words:

> By faith Abraham, when called to go to a place he would later receive as his inheritance, obeyed and went, *even though he did not know where he was going* (emphasis mine).[4]

Suddenly a light dawned, not the bolt out of the blue, not an overwhelming Presence, not even unspeakable joy, but simply a subtle assurance that to this day has never left me. Suddenly I realized that as God called, Abraham obeyed. Faith was both hearing and acting. I had sensed that God's call was upon my life—the hearing. It was now time for acting. Believe it or not, I had never read the Bible. I'm not absolutely certain that I could have named the four Gospels. I decided to attend a graduate school of theology knowing full well that the biggest revelation to me would be my own stupidity. I knew nothing of theology and even less about church history. Then came the gradual realization that I wanted to spend the rest of my life in some kind of ministry. Even though I did not know where I was going, I was getting excited, really excited.

### In Times of Transition

This morning I spent time in the book of Leviticus. I read about the deaths of Aaron's two oldest sons. As the nation Israel prepared to begin worshiping in the newly constructed Tent of Meeting, Nadab and Abihu entered the Tabernacle with unauthorized fire. "So fire came out from the presence of the LORD and consumed them, and they died before the LORD" (Lev. 10:2). Isn't that a bit harsh? I remember similar feelings about poor Uzzah who died reaching out to steady the Ark of the Covenant when the oxen stumbled and the cart was about to overturn (2 Sam. 6:6-7). That did not seem like a very big sin. Surely he woke up in Abraham's bosom. The point is that *during times of transition, God is a stickler for detail.* So much is at stake. Like instructions for the surgeon's scalpel, we had better get it right. There is irony here, however. Too often during times of transition we are so consumed by the transition that we miss the detail, and our best opportunities for life and ministry can slip by unnoticed.

I was in transition. Every day I was learning things that would change the way I thought, believed and behaved forever. Those were heady days. Then it was time for another decision. Now that I had completed degrees in theology, should I return to my more secular ambitions as a form of ministry, or should I pursue a different path altogether? I prayed about it. I did not want to be oblivious to the detail and miss any signposts of warning or promise. Over weeks I began to realize that perhaps God was leading me into full-time Christian service. I was fortunate enough to receive a scholarship for study abroad, and since I already had two master's degrees, why not a Ph.D.? I traveled to England and received still another scholarship from Trinity College at the University of Bristol.

As I completed the terminal degree I learned even more about prayer while researching the history and theology of Christian mysticism. I completed the degree on my 27th birthday. What now? Life was still one step at a time—constant transition. I needed to pay attention. Perhaps I should be a pastor. Once again I prayed, but this time I knew enough to enlist the prayers of others.

### Prayer as a Certain Guide

"How can I know my choice of career?" Pray. "How can I know if this is the right person to marry?" Pray. "How can I choose the right church? Pray. "How can I make the everyday kinds of choices that will best benefit my family and friends?" Pray. "How can I be a loving and supportive spouse?" Pray. "How can I know the will of God?" Pray.

I cannot tell you what prayer has meant to me over the years. Last night I had dinner with a prominent surgeon. He is a wonderful man of prayer. Halfway through the meal I told him one of the secrets to my relationship with a living God. In recent days I've learned to spend more and more time with the devout, especially children and grandmothers, orphans and nuns. Last year I was in Pittsburgh and early on a Sunday morning I was introduced to a classroom of children, four through six year-olds. Twenty or so gathered around me, laid hands on me and prayed that God would bless my sermon. I've never been so anointed. Rarely do I go anywhere any more without asking the children to pray.

Jesus says, "I tell you the truth, unless you change and become like little children, you will never enter the kingdom of heaven. Therefore, whoever humbles himself like this child is the greatest in the kingdom of heaven" (Matt. 18:3-4). So now I ask churches to gather the children to pray for me before I preach.

### The Child and the Inquisitor General

I once found a story of a small girl who had visions of Jesus during the time of the Spanish Inquisition.[5] The Inquisitors did not like for little girls to have visions of Jesus, since it was assumed that Jesus spoke only to the leaders of the Church. The Inquisitor General called her before the Tribunal to intimidate her. At one point the Inquisitor scoffed, "The next time you see Jesus ask him what sin I confessed at my last confessional." The little girl nodded. The next week she was once again called before the Tribunal. "Well, did you see Jesus?" She nodded. "Did you ask him what sin I confessed at my last confessional?" Again, she nodded. "And what did he say?" With hands folded calmly in her lap she looked up at him, "Jesus says, 'Tell the man to read Jeremiah 31:34.[6] Then tell the man that I forget.'" As I was thinking about that story, suddenly I caught an image of that little girl as she was standing before the Inquisitor General. In my mind she was surrounded by a host of angels. These angels were huge and intimidating (little wonder whenever the Bible speaks of angels it says, "Fear not"). They had tattoos and wore Nikes. Then, as I looked closer, I realized that every one of them was carrying a millstone with words similar to those of Luke 17:2 chiseled around the edges, "If anyone would cause any of these little ones to stumble, let a millstone be placed about his neck and dropped to the bottom of the sea."

John Wesley fully understood the value of children. In his *Instructions for Children* he writes at length about their special care lest our prayers be hindered.[7]

I love nursing homes. Some people close to the end of life have recovered their childlikeness. At the church on the southside of Chicago, I was expected to visit nursing homes and shut-ins. I shall never forget Mrs. Cameron. The first time I walked into her room she was restless. She was bedridden, covered with bedsores, and her tongue was so swollen that she could not speak, only grunt. Fortunately her daughter was there and could interpret her grunts. Through her daughter she pleaded with me, "Pray that I die." Although I would probably respond to that request differently now, I reacted, "What do you mean? God won't take you until God is through with you." She looked surprised, "I've not been out of bed for over two years. I can't even talk." I retorted, "You can think, and if you can think you can pray, and if you can pray, you can pray for the likes of me. God knows I need it. I promise to visit you every week if you will pray for me." We fell in love in that moment. Her daughter told me that praying for me was about all she did for the next two years. As I preached her funeral I said to everyone present, "If I've had any success as your pastor it is because of the prayers of Mrs. Cameron." To this day I believe that with all my heart.

The Beatitudes contain "antitheses." These establish what I've already mentioned as the first principle of Jesus. If you want to gain life, give it up. If you want to be great, be a servant. If you want to be first, be last. Perhaps most important is that in the New Testament weakness is not so much something to be overcome, it is the place where God dwells. So where do we lose this childlike innocence? It began in the garden. The point of the story of Adam and Eve is that when we sin, we lose the ability to perceive reality beyond the senses. Fortunately, we can gain it back in old age. Both of my parents, just before they died, were more aware of what was going on beyond the veil than within the veil.

I also recall that as a young seminary professor I met Agnes Sanford, a godly woman of prayer. For some reason she and her housemate, Edith Drury, took a liking to me. They had me over for dinner on several occasions. Since many of my students were older than I was, these women tended to worry about me. On several occasions Edith would attend my classes, sit quietly in a corner with her head bowed and eyes closed, and pray for me the entire hour while I lectured. Not once did a single student ask, "What's up with the old woman in the corner?" I am a blessed man.

### Let's Talk about Your Future

What about the future? Here is a passage from Jeremiah, one of my favorite Old Testament authors,

> This is what the LORD says: "When seventy years are completed for Babylon, I will come to you and fulfill my gracious promise to bring you back to this place. For I know the plans

> I have for you," declares the LORD, "plans to prosper you and not to harm you, *plans to give you hope and a future* [emphasis mine]. Then you will call upon me and come and pray to me, and I will listen to you. You will seek me and find me when you seek me with all your heart (Jer. 29:10-13).

That was a word of prophecy that would one day give encouragement to those in exile, whether they be in Babylon or Bangkok or Chicago or Cape Town or London or Lagos or Paris or Pyong Yang. If you seek God with all your heart, God plans to give you hope and a future. Whether you are as young as Moses in the bulrushes or as old as Methuselah, believe it with all your heart. Trust God for a vision. After all, if you can describe your vision, I can predict your future.

**End Notes**

[1] Dan. 5:25-28.
[2] John Wesley, *Works* (Vol. 1, p. 102 of the Jackson ed.).
[3] An email from Molly Warren.
[4] Hebrews 11:8 (emphasis mine).
[5] It grieves me to have to mention the Inquisition. In Spain it had somewhat of a different character than in the rest of the Church. Begun in the early thirteenth century as a judicial apparatus to bring heretics back into the fold—especially the Catharists—inquisitors had been recruited, largely among the Dominicans. By the end of the fifteenth century, the Inquisition in Spain was closely bound to state. Set up with Papal approval by Ferdinand and Isabella, it was originally directed against the *marranos*—baptized Jews suspected of having returned to their old beliefs and practice; the *moriscos*—Moors who had been force to accept baptism, the *Alumbrados* or *Illuminati*—a loosed-knit group of spiritual persons who claimed visions and

revelations; and Protestants. By 1516 it was highly centralized and organized under a single Inquisitor General. As time advanced, the penalties increased from excommunication, to confiscated property, to torture, to burning at the stake. Between 1481 and 1498, the Inquisitor General, a Dominican prior named Tomás de Torquemada, condemned, imprisoned or executed 120,000 Spanish intellectuals and Jews with fanatical zeal. At least 2,000 were burned at the stake. Then, toward the end of the sixteenth century the Inquisition was extended to the New World. Reportedly 120,000 were burned in Peru. The smell of burning flesh must have reminded them of their old pagan sacrifices.

[6] Jeremiah 31:34 speaks of the new covenant where God "will forgive their wickedness and will remember their sins no more."

[7] Albert C. Outler, *The Works of John Wesley*. Volume 3. Nashville: Abingdon Press, 1986.

## Chapter Eleven

# "What About the Unforgivable Sin?"

### (Can God's Call on My Life Be Renewed?)

Many of my students now are second career. Some heard God's call years before but are just now responding. Most of them ask these or related questions, "Is it too late? Must I now settle for God's second best?" I respond that I believe the perfect will of God is constantly being refreshed and renewed. You never have to settle for God's second best because God has no second best. Certainly sin has its consequences, but I also believe that if God calls you to Los Angeles, and you go to New York, then God has a perfect will for your return from New York. God is that kind of a God.

Let me illustrate. Let's say that you know that God wants you to get in your car and drive to a neighborhood shelter, where you will spend the next couple of days working with the homeless. You say, "Lord, I appreciate the invitation and I know that kind of thing is important, but you're going to have to give me a rain check. You know what I'm facing this week with appointments and deadlines. There is just no way I can get it all done if I go and attempt to do ministry at a homeless shelter." So for the next twenty-four hours you live in the hell of disobedience (I trust I'm not the only one who knows that feeling). Finally, the next day you say, "OK, God, I hope you're happy. I'm tired of being miserable so I'm going."

If you understand the principles of law and grace, the law says that for the rest of your sweet life you're going to be twenty-four hours behind the perfect will of God, while grace says, the moment you decide to obey God, get in your car and act upon it (although you've missed the joy and satisfaction of twenty-four hours of meaningful ministry); you are at that moment where you would have been had you obeyed God twenty-four hours earlier. You want chapter and verse? Look no further than the parable of the vineyard owner who hired some in the morning, some midmorning, some at noon, some in the mid-afternoon, and some in the evening (Matt. 20:1-16). It is once again the story of the prodigal.

God really is a God of fresh starts and new beginnings. The photograph at the head of the chapter is of flowers growing in front of a war-torn, bullet-ridden building in the midst of a town that is coming back to life, better than before.

### The Unforgivable Sin

Doubt frequently wonders about the unforgivable sin. Have I gone too far? Let me speak to that. Jesus says,

> . . . every sin and blasphemy will be forgiven men, but the blasphemy against the Spirit will not be forgiven. Anyone who speaks a word against the Son of Man will be forgiven, but anyone who speaks against the Holy Spirit will not be forgiven, either in this age or in the age to come (Matt. 12:31-32).

In the context for that passage the Pharisees had just attributed the power of Jesus to the power of Beelzebub (Matt. 12:24). Jesus had predicted the topsy-turvy kind of a world where everything good becomes evil, and everything evil becomes good. We suspected that possibility earlier when discussing God's judgment against the inhabitants of Sodom and Gomorrah. People will actually persecute the Church thinking they are doing the will of God. The implication is this: The unforgivable sin—grieving the Holy Spirit—is not a particular sin; it is a disposition of mind and spirit. It relates to people who have sinned away every ounce of good that is in them so that there is no longer any good left to respond to God. God never turns on us; we turn on God, utterly, unforgivably. Now, having said that, I don't know that I've met more than one or two persons in my lifetime that I suspected were that wide of the mark (sin literally means to "miss the mark"). In other words, if you are reading these words I can assure you that you have NOT committed the unforgivable sin. Those people do not pick up books like this.

**Is It Too Late?**

OK, there's still hope, but here's yet another question. "I sensed God's call on my life years ago, but I've resisted ever since. Now I'm at a different place in my life and I think I might be ready. Is it too late? Since I gave up on plan A, can I settle for plan B?"

Let me tell you a story. When God delivered the children of Israel from the Egyptian oppressor, they first settled around Mount Sinai, during which time they got organized and received the law, not once, but twice. After eighteen months or so God called them to take the land promised to Abraham and his descendants. All they had to do was to trust God alone and obey the laws and ordinances. Then the land was theirs.

The distance to the southern reaches of the land was only an eleven-day walk, but there were two million Israelites, so it

## CHAPTER 11: "WHAT ABOUT THE UNFORGIVABLE SIN?" 143

took the better part of two months to make the trek. When they arrived within sight the decision was made to send twelve spies into the land to measure the enemy's strength to resist such an invasion. Of the twelve spies, ten returned with a bad report. "Yes, it is a land of milk and honey but the resistance will be fierce. There are giants in the land, and in comparison we seem like grasshoppers." The majority report carried the day, and the people were discouraged. When telling this story I sometimes offer a $100 bill to anyone who can name just one of the ten who came back with a bad report. Although they are all named in Numbers 13, no one has ever claimed the prize. All ten died of a plague within days. Only Joshua and Caleb survived because they were the only ones to return with a good report.

> Joshua son of Nun and Caleb son of Jephunneh, who were among those who had explored the land, tore their clothes and said to the entire Israelite assembly, "The land we passed through and explored is exceedingly good. If the LORD is pleased with us, he will lead us into that land, a land flowing with milk and honey, and will give it to us. Only do not rebel against the LORD. And do not be afraid of the people of the land, because we will swallow them up. Their protection is gone, but the LORD is with us. Do not be afraid of them" (Num. 14:6-9).

Even though some took courage and made a feeble attempt to enter the land, it was too little too late, and they were soundly defeated. God had already sentenced the rest of the nation to thirty-eight more years in the desert sands. During that time an entire generation died out. The only ones over twenty-one who had escaped from Egypt to enter the land forty years later were Joshua and Caleb.

So, a generation later the nation was once again poised on the border of the land, this time on the plains of Moab. Once again, God said, "Take the land." Once again the people were reluctant. Many complained (no doubt the Back-to-Egypt Committee), "Since we did not experience your first call thirty-eight years ago, we are working from memory here. Are you certain the contract is still valid, the covenant is still on?" Pay attention to what God does by way of reply.

Balak, the king of Moab, was nervous about what to do with all these Israelites camped on his plains. There were too many to fight. Then he got an idea, "I'll send word to the internationally known pagan prophet, Balaam. He will come and curse them for me and they will leave."

When Balak's men approached Balaam, he was reluctant. "I've no quarrel with these Israelites." Balak was so insistent, however, that Balaam finally agreed to saddle his donkey and make the trip. At one point the prophet and his donkey approached a narrow place in the road, rimmed with cavernous walls. At the end of the narrows an angel of the Lord stood with drawn sword. The prophet did not see the angel, but the donkey did and understandably balked. The prophet began beating the donkey, but the donkey was so frightened that he moved to the side of the wall, scraping the prophet's leg, and eventually sat down. As the prophet continued to beat the donkey, the Lord opened the donkey's mouth. It should be noted that the donkey did not say anything terribly profound (we give that donkey far too much press) but he did say words to the effect, "Listen old son, don't you realize that I'm out of character here? Have I ever sat down on you before?" When the prophet conceded that point, suddenly (and here is the real miracle) the Lord opened the prophet's eyes, and the prophet saw the angel as well. The Angel said, "Go, but speak only what I tell you to speak."

As Balaam approached Moab he was met by Balak, who expected him to curse the Israelites. Whenever the prophet opened his mouth, however, blessings, not curses, came tumbling out,

> How can I curse those whom God has not cursed?... Who can count the dust of Jacob or number the fourth part of Israel? Let me die the death of the righteous, and may my end be like theirs (Num. 23:8, 10)!

This was only the first of seven (count them) blessings. Understandably Balak reacted, "What have you done to me? I brought you to curse my enemies but you have done nothing but bless them" (Num. 23:11). In effect, this is what God was saying to answer the questions of the Israelites regarding the validity of the ancient covenant:

> I am still with you!
> I am still with you!
> I am still with you!
> I am still with you!
> I am still with you!
> I am still with you!
> I am still with you!

So, cross the Jordan and take the land promised to your father Abraham!

*Here's a point of relevancy for your own personal dilemma.* If God knows everything, then God knew that when this story was written you would be reading it thousands of years later. It should not, therefore, be too much of a stretch to believe that God had you in mind when this story was written. So take it personally. I know, many of you feel as if you have flopped around desert sands for thirty-eight years or more, but God would say, "I am still with you! The contract is still valid! The covenant is still on! Fulfill my call upon your life! Rise up and take the land!" That's what faith does when it wants to overcome doubt. Here's something else that faith does.

**Faith Goes Fishing**

Luke 5 tells a wonderful story of the inevitable crowd pressing against Jesus, looking for a word from on high. At one point Jesus is backed up to the sea, but sees Peter cleaning his nets next to an empty boat. To gain better perspective from which to teach, he asks Peter to row him a short distance from the shore. Peter agrees, but all the while Jesus is teaching, Peter is in the back of the boat grumbling, "Fished all night and caught nothing. Fished all night and caught nothing." Finally, Jesus turns to Peter and says. "Peter, if fish is what's really important to you, row out into the deep. I'll show you fish." Jesus spoke with such authority that before the left side of Peter's brain could object, "I'm a fisherman and caught nothing; what does this carpenter know about fishing?" he found himself rowing.

The waters of the Sea of Galilee are so clear that fish can see the nets during the daylight hours, so most fishing must be done at night. Still, Peter rowed and when he threw out the nets they were instantly full of fish, so full that he had to call for James and John to bring another boat to hold the catch. Overwhelmed, Peter fell at Jesus' feet, "Go away from me, Lord; I am a sinful man." When the boats were brought back to shore, Jesus said an interesting thing, "Don't be afraid; from now on you will catch men." Peter must have been thinking, "Fishers of men? If we caught them, what would we do with them?"

At that point a parallel passage suggests that Jesus says, "Follow me," and walks out toward the horizon leaving Peter halfway between himself and two boats filled with fish. Peter looks back at those fish (that's what life is all about for a fisherman), and he looks ahead at Jesus. He looks back at those fish (not one, but two boats filled to overflowing), and he looks ahead at Jesus. He looks back at those fish (food and supplies for a month), and he looks ahead at Jesus. Finally, he looks ahead at Jesus, the Son of the living God, and his life changes forever.

**God's Call**

I once heard a sermon preached by my student and friend, Kent Reynolds, on Bezalel and Oholiab. These were the men chosen by God to build the Tent of Meeting.

> Then Moses said to the Israelites, "See, the LORD has chosen Bezalel son of Uri, the son of Hur, of the tribe of Judah, and he has filled him with the Spirit of God, with skill, ability and knowledge in all kinds of crafts—to make artistic designs for work in gold, silver and bronze, to cut and set stones, to work in wood and to engage in all kinds of artistic craftsmanship. And he has given both him and Oholiab son of Ahisamach, of the tribe of Dan, the ability to teach others. He has filled them with skill to do all kinds of work as craftsmen, designers, embroiderers in blue, purple and scarlet yarn and fine linen, and weavers—all of them master craftsmen and designers. So Bezalel, Oholiab and every skilled person to whom the LORD has given skill and ability to know how to carry out all the work of constructing the sanctuary are to do the work just as the LORD has commanded (Ex. 35:30-36:1).

When you think about it, that is a pretty amazing passage. Let me break it down. First, God called them while they were still in the loins of their ancestors—"son of Uri, the son of Hur, of the tribe of Judah." Like the sons of Aaron for the priesthood, God had these carpenters in mind for generations.

Second, God filled them with the Spirit. In spite of the fact that there is no general outpouring of the Spirit under the old covenant, God does call, and then fill, specific people for specific tasks. We see it in kings, priests and prophets. We see it in Hannah, Esther and Deborah. We see it in Bezalel, Oholiab and a whole host of people who were skilled with certain crafts.

Third—and here's the clincher—they were gifted to teach others. God rarely does things by addition. God almost always works by multiplication. Bezalel and Oholiab could never have done all of the work by themselves. Jethro, the father-in-law of Moses, taught him as much when it came to judging the disputes of the people. "Why do you alone sit as judge....What you are doing is not good. You and these people who come to you will only wear yourselves out. The work is too heavy for you; you cannot handle it alone" (Ex. 18:14,18).

Kent Reynolds insists that good leaders allow people to fail. Our natural sphere of influence usually determines our supernatural gifts. God delights in turning our natural talents into supernatural gifts when it comes to training or encouraging others for ministry, whether it's healing the sick or driving a nail. Good leaders rarely say, "Go over there and sit down; just don't touch anything." They say, "Here, try this. You can do it. I will help you."

Fourth, all they had to do was to do it "just as the LORD has commanded," that is, under the direction and leadership of God. I love it when Jesus says,

> Come to me, all you who are weary and burdened, and I will give you rest. Take my yoke upon you and learn from me, for I am gentle and humble in heart, and you will find rest for your souls. For my yoke is easy and my burden is light (Matt. 11:28-30).

## Where Do I Go from Here?

At some point we need to take an assessment of where we are in all of this. Am I still running from God? I once attended a retreat for college students. An old man was there (about my age). When we were introduced, he proudly announced that he was the "resident seeker." I asked, "How long have you been seeking?" He said, "About forty years." The directness of my response surprised even me, "You're not seeking; you're running. At some point *not to decide is to decide.* If I had been looking for something for forty years and not found it, I'd start looking somewhere else."

Here's a challenge—an honest wager. Where do you go from here? May I anticipate your response?

*Let's see if I have this straight. It does not matter what I've done. It does not matter how far I've run. If I'm reading this book, then I've not committed the unforgivable sin. And God can renew a call upon my life and give me meaning and purpose just as significant as if I had obeyed God thirty years ago. Right? Now, all I have to do is stop running, listen to what God is saying, and then commit all that I know of myself to all that I know of God. Right? If I repent, that is, grieve over the separation my sin has caused, God will forgive me and take my sin from me. Right? Finally, if I put my faith and trust in Jesus Christ at the point of that repentance, then the Spirit of God will bear witness with my spirit that I am a child of God, and I can find peace. Right? That's the honest wager. Right? You would stake your life on it. Right? Then let's do it!*

Your life would change forever.

## Chapter Twelve

# "Is Faith in Jesus Christ the Only Way to Heaven?"
## (The Perennial Question)

May I confess that I do not particularly like this question, but inquiring minds (honest doubters) want to know. In fact, this question from a different perspective has already been addressed in the chapter, "Why Jesus?" So, let me ask it in a slightly different form. If faith in Jesus Christ really is the only way to heaven, and if God really is no respecter of persons (i.e., if God does not love some peoples more than other peoples), shouldn't God give every man, woman and child the world over an equal opportunity to respond, if not to the name, at least to the person of Jesus Christ? Makes sense to me.

Now, admittedly, while I've not yet worked all of that out theologically, honest doubt keeps pushing the issue even further. Why isn't it enough simply to be faithful to what you were taught to believe (in some instances from infancy with little or no exposure to anything else)? Why not say, "Well, if it works for you!" or, "So long as you are sincere!" Let me try to explain.

I believe that it is faith in Jesus Christ alone that puts us right with God, that heals the brokenness of our time, and makes us fit to share the heritage of God's glory. I've had students react to such a statement, "How can you be so narrow-minded as to believe in the uniqueness of faith in Jesus Christ?" My response, "Listen, my believing in the uniqueness of faith in Jesus Christ may not make me right, but it sure makes me an evangelist." Here's why.

**An Impasse**

It is important at the beginning to realize that Christianity (right or wrong) is far more than a philosophy of life; it is a *way of life*.[1] It is a relationship with a living God, and if you attempt to reduce the Christian faith to a system of do's and don'ts, then one religion is about as good as another. In a few words, I believe that Christianity picks up where every other religion leaves off.

That is not to say that I am right, and the rest of the world is wrong. If God is a Triangle (and I think God is a circle), God does not become a circle to accommodate who I believe God to be. God remains a Triangle. Furthermore, truth has never changed to accommodate what I believe truth to be. Truth is truth, regardless of what I might think it happens to be. Having said that, never accuse me of two minds. If you could convince me that I am wrong, you could pour me into a basket. Flesh would not cling to bone any longer. I'm a dead man. That's how much of me is at stake. It is just that I know of no other way to access the power of the Holy Spirit that enables me to overcome. We have stated time and again, the Bible teaches that repentance and faith in Jesus Christ alone puts us right with God. No other religion believes that to be true. At some point integrity reaches an impasse. We may all be wrong but we cannot all be right. We disagree.

I am sometimes asked, "What are the non-negotiables?" Again, my reply, "There are no non-negotiables when it comes to sharing my faith with peoples of other faiths." I will put Jesus Christ on any table, around the world—even up. I am not into Christianity for the pain. It's just that I know of no other way to live an abundant life. If you have something that does it better than Jesus, love me enough to let me in on your secret. You may have a convert.

All of this is not to say, however, that I have no non-negotiables when it comes to defining what it means to be a Christian. Certainly I do—read on and I hope some of those will become apparent.

**What Does It Mean to Be a Christian?**

The Christian faith is the interaction, *balance and union of propositional and experiential truth.* It is never enough just to make sense. A part of shortening the leap is creating the kind of environment where leaping into the unknown beats all the alternatives, where trusting Jesus Christ alone promises to deliver us from all the distractions that would attempt to consume us.

So, what is the *propositional truth*? From the Prologue of the Gospel of John, Jesus is described as fully God and fully man. Jesus "was the Word, and the Word was with God, and the Word was God." Follow that with "the Word became flesh and made his dwelling among us. We have seen his glory, the glory of the One and Only, who came from the Father, full of grace and truth" (John 1:1, 14).

From the words of Jesus himself it is clear that he knew himself to be unique in his relationship with God and creation. Note those wonderful "I am" passages in John. "I am the bread of life. He who comes to me will never go hungry . . ."

## CHAPTER 12: "IS FAITH IN JESUS CHRIST THE ONLY WAY TO HEAVEN?"

(John 6:35). "I am the light of the world. Whoever follows me will never walk in darkness..." (John 8:12). "I am the gate; whoever enters through me will be saved" (John 10:9). "I am the good shepherd. The good shepherd lays down his life for the sheep" (John 10:11). "I am the resurrection and the life. He who believes in me will live, even though he dies" (John 11:25). "I am the way and the truth and the life. No one comes to the Father except through me" (John 14:6). "I am the true vine.... No branch can bear fruit by itself...." (John 15:1, 4).

Follow that with the words Peter preached before the Sanhedrin in response to their inquiry regarding the healing of the crippled beggar, "By what power or what name did you do this?" Peter replied,

> It is by the name Jesus Christ of Nazareth, whom you crucified but whom God raised from the dead, that this man stands before you healed. He is "the stone you builders rejected, which has become the capstone." Salvation is found in no one else, for there is no other name under heaven given to men by which we must be saved (Acts 4:10-12).

It should be apparent from these and many other similar passages that to be a Christian is to affirm the basic content of the creeds that Christians the world over recite in their services of worship week after week. For example, here is the oldest and the most well known.

> I believe in God the Father Almighty, maker of heaven and earth; and in Jesus Christ his only Son our Lord: who was conceived by the Holy Spirit, born of the Virgin Mary, suffered under Pontius Pilate, was crucified, dead, and buried; he descended into hell. The third day he rose

> from the dead; he ascended into heaven, and sits
> at the right hand of God the Father Almighty;
> from thence he shall come to judge the quick
> and the dead. I believe in the Holy Spirit, the
> holy catholic church, the communion of saints,
> the forgiveness of sins, the resurrection of the
> body, and the life everlasting.[2]

"You mean I have to believe all of that to be a Christian, even the Virgin Birth?" It depends on what you mean by "believe the Virgin Birth." If by not believing you are saying that Jesus Christ is not the Son of God, but only an impostor, that is problematic. If you are denying the authenticity of Scripture, that too is problematic. In Luke 1:34 when the angel announces to Mary that she will give birth to a son, she clearly states, "How will this be . . . since I am a virgin?"

On the other hand, if you are saying that it makes better sense to you to believe that the Son of God was conceived by a human father, and the image of the Virgin Birth is an interesting way of communicating his duel nature metaphorically, that perhaps is another matter.

As for me, the Virgin Birth makes perfect sense, and I see no reason to deny it. Even in plane geometry when two independent planes intersect (the Holy Spirit and Mary), the point or place of intersection is always a straight line. Having said that, I know many wonderful Christians who fully affirm both the deity and humanity of Jesus Christ who have never even considered such a doctrine, true or false.

So what of the *experiential truth*? Christians are fond of saying, "The Devil believes in God and in all of the truths of Christianity." To become a Christian is obviously more than intellectual ascent to propositional truth. It involves a personal commitment. It means that we not only believe but are willing to also trust him with our lives as well. I recall a story where a famous aerialist amazed the crowds by the way he could dance across a wire strung between two tall buildings. At one point he took a wheelbarrow to the platform and asked the throngs below, "Do you believe that I can roll this wheelbarrow across the wire?" They all shouted, "Yes, we believe." He then proceeded to do so with apparent ease. Then he asked, "Do you believe that I can roll a man in the wheelbarrow across the wire?" Once again they all shouted, "Yes, we believe." He then asked, "Who will volunteer?" He got no takers. It is one thing to believe but quite another to volunteer. *At some point the leap of faith volunteers.*

So, being a Christian means *believing* and *committing*, but it also means *speaking* and *doing*. Let's look now at speaking. *Christianity is personal but never private.* Jesus says, "If anyone is ashamed of me and my words, the Son of Man will be ashamed of him when he comes in his glory and in the glory of the Father and of the holy angels" (Luke 9:26). Further on he says, "I tell you, whoever acknowledges me before men, the Son of Man will also acknowledge him before the angels of God. But he who disowns me before men will be disowned before the angels of God" (Luke 12:8-9).

### Ain't No Rock Gonna Take My Place!

I love the old African-American spiritual, "Ain't No Rock Gonna Take My Place!" Those of you who know the story of the Pharisees ordering Jesus to rebuke his disciples for praising God upon his triumphal entry into Jerusalem will remember these words, "I tell you, . . . if they keep quiet, the stones will cry out" (Luke 19:40).

It has been stated that you can put the good news of Jesus Christ into principles of supply and demand, and be well assured that the demand is out there. If people in your village are starving, what do you do? Unless you are a brick, you feed them. If people in your town are naked, what do you do? Unless you are a stone, you clothe them. If people in your city are in bondage to the things that would attempt to swallow them, what do you do? Unless you just do not understand the principle, you tell them about the power of the Holy Spirit available through personal faith in Jesus Christ. Now tell me, what part of that ministry would you want to leave out? We do not apologize for feeding the hungry or clothing the naked, so why should we apologize for sharing the good news of the gospel that can set people free from "the sin that so easily entangles them" (Heb. 12:1)?

May I repeat that my believing I am right does NOT make the rest of the world my enemy? It does, however, compel me to share my understanding of the gospel with anyone who will listen. In the next chapter we will talk further about just what it means to share the gospel and how we can overcome potential barriers to Spirit-assisted evangelism. For now, however, simply know that it is important to speak a redemptive word to the next generation.

**Doing the Gospel**

It is not only important to believe, to commit and to speak, but also to do the gospel in order to be a Christian. The Church not only has an apologetic, but it *is* also an apologetic. John Wesley insisted, "You cannot be saved by works, but you cannot be saved without them either. Methodists who do not fulfill all righteousness deserve the hottest place in the lake of fire." For Wesley faith had its inevitable fruit. He was quick to quote, "Make a tree good and its fruit will be good, or make a tree bad and its fruit will be bad, for a tree is recognized by its fruit" (Matt. 12:33). I don't care if it looks like a grapevine; if it produces apples, call it an apple tree. The apostle John in the book of Revelation insisted that when he observed the return of Christ in a vision, "The dead were judged according to what they had done as recorded in the books" (Rev. 20:12). Doesn't that imply works-righteousness? Certainly not when you realize that the ability to do all good works is only by the grace of God. "For it is by grace you have been saved, through

## CHAPTER 12: "IS FAITH IN JESUS CHRIST THE ONLY WAY TO HEAVEN?"

faith—and this not from yourselves, it is the gift of God—not by works, so that no one can boast" (Eph. 2:8-9a).

Just as some honest doubters are turned off by "Jesus only" slogans that seemingly condemn the rest of the world with apparent relish, they are also turned off by Christian hypocrisy. Let me be quick to add that becoming a Christian does not make a hypocrite, a non-hypocrite; it makes him less hypocritical. Nor does becoming a Christian make that Christian better than non-Christians; it makes her better than what she was. Some of my non-Christian friends are far easier to get along with than some of my Christian friends. But, if my Christian friends are hard to get along with now, you should have seen them before. So, how do I do the gospel?

I've always believed that a good place to start is with feeding the hungry, clothing the naked and visiting the sick and imprisoned (Isa. 58:6-9). We have spoken several times about meeting the needs of the poor. What about the poor in your own neighborhood? When I go out to teach and preach on weekend missions (which I do once a month), I inform the churches that if they will give ten percent of their gross income to the poor in the neighborhoods where they live for at least one year, I will come without honorarium. I've had only one taker in thirty years. If God expects the church member to tithe, why wouldn't God expect the church body to tithe as well?

Doing the gospel also relates to our attitude toward others. Once again Jesus is our model. On the eve of his crucifixion Jesus took off his outer clothing, wrapped a towel around his waist and washed the feet of his disciples. Later he explained,

> Now that I, your Lord and Teacher, have washed your feet, you also should wash one another's feet. I have set you an example that you should do as I have done for you (John 13:14-15).

Surely, if you know who you are and have nothing to hide

or prove, you can take off your "outer clothing" (any façade) and become a servant of God's creation.

Jesus loved his enemies. He forgave sinners. He had compassion for the oppressed. He condemned injustice. He healed the sick. He fed the hungry. He did all of those things that endear him to Christians and non-Christians alike the world over. He said of himself,

> The Spirit of the Lord is on me,
> because he has anointed me
> to preach good news to the poor.
> He has sent me to proclaim freedom for
> the prisoners
> and recovery of sight for the blind,
> to release the oppressed,
> to proclaim the year of the Lord's favor
> (Luke 4:18-19).[3]

Honest doubt says, "But that was Jesus. How can we expect to do the things that Jesus did?" Jesus speaks to that as well,

> I tell you the truth, anyone who has faith in me will do what I have been doing. He will *do even greater things,* than these, because I am going to the Father. And I will do whatever you ask in my name, so that the Son may bring glory to the Father, You may ask me for anything *in my name* and I will do it (John 14:12-14, emphasis mine).

Obviously, this quotation raises two important questions. First, how did Jesus do the things that he did? Second, what does he mean by the phrase, "in my name?"

I sometimes ask the question, "How is it that Jesus worked all those wonderful miracles?" The usual response is, "He was the Son of God." Yes, but while the Son of God dwelt among us he was fully human, just as you and I are fully human. He emptied himself (Phil. 2:7). He left all those "omni" characteristics behind. He was not omnipresent; He was not omniscient; He was not omnipotent. He was mortal (Mk. 15:37). He was tempted (Heb. 2:18). In fact, the only way he could do all those miracles was to access the power of the Holy Spirit, the same Holy Spirit power available to us today. In fact, in community we can do even greater things than He did as we seek to extend his ministry until his return (John 14:12). Let God arise!

So what about the phrase, "in my name." First, that is not a magical incantation. "In my name" simply means consistent with the mind of Jesus. In fact, if our heart's desire (that which consumes us) is consistent with the mind of Jesus, then that, by its very nature, becomes a perpetual prayer that guarantees an anointing, a blessing from on high. Again, let God arise!

I love it when Christians do the things they are called to do. They always make me proud. They make the best case for moving honest doubt to enduring faith. Let me give you a wonderful example.

### A Friend in Bangalore

My wife and I have a friend in India. Her name is Tammy Hutchins; we call her Tammy Ma. After an incredibly difficult childhood Tammy became a Christian through the Wesley Foundation at the University of Georgia. Upon graduation she felt called to India, and after a year of seminary went to Bangalore, quite on her own. She walked the busy streets until she understood a need. She encountered hundreds of children orphaned by AIDS. Building a ministry purely by faith (she refuses to ask anyone for money), remarkably she now has made a home called *Kirubai* for more than forty such children.[4] Once we were privileged to sit in on a brief devotional for twenty or so of the girls as they prepared for bed. Tammy Ma described situations where the girls might feel the need to pray. She told them there were two very special words that could make all the difference in the world. If they were lost and needed to find their way home, pray the words. If they were worried about a difficult project at school, pray the words. If they were lonely or sad and needed a friend, pray the words. If they were sick and needed someone to care, pray the words. If they were hurt by family or friend and needed grace to forgive, pray the words. As she continued to describe more and more situations where the two special words could deliver, the girls begged and pleaded, "Tell us the words, Tammy Ma, tell us the words!" Finally she spoke, "Jesus, help!" "Jesus, help *me*!" would work as well. Let God arise, indeed.

**End Notes**

[1] It is interesting that many Muslims also insist that Islam is not a religion, it is a *din* (a way of life).

[2] The Apostles' Creed probably dates back to the mid-second century.

[3] cf. Isaiah 61:1-2.

[4] Since Tammy Hutchins refuses to ask for money, and if you should feel so led, the Mission sponsor in the U.S.A. is Wesley Fellowship Partners, P.O. Box 1203, Marietta, GA 30061.

## CHAPTER THIRTEEN

# "WHAT ABOUT THE NEXT GENERATION?"
## (OVERCOMING BARRIERS TO SPIRIT-ASSISTED MINISTRY)

In the background above are sculptures depicting people (on the right) bypassing suffering humanity (on the left). The foreground reveals a similar scene, only in real time. If you have come into a saving experience of Jesus Christ you might be wondering, "How can *I* do ministry for the next generation?" At some point, many Christians ask that question with the following comments, "Let someone else do that. That's just not my gift. I'll write a check."

### How Am I Doing?

We have already described Christianity as believing, committing, talking and doing. Since the principles discussed below relate to all aspects of Christian ministry, for the sake of time and space let's look at talking. For most Christians that's the most difficult.

In an introductory courses on evangelism I always give this assignment: Develop case studies from conversations about faith in Jesus Christ with three unchurched (or at least dechurched) people. I know this is a bit of a gimmick but—if needed—I even give them a way to ease into the experience.

> Explain to these persons that you are taking a course in evangelism and in order to pass you must speak with three different people about faith in Christ with the expectation that they will then critique your presentation as to whether or not it makes sense. As a novice evangelist, you need to know, "How am I doing?"

Although the results are sometimes amazing, I cannot tell you how difficult this is for most—even in seminary. So why would I make such an assignment? Most have never once had such an experience, and although this is certainly not the best approach to evangelism—it smacks of hit and run—at least it gets them moving. So, why the resistance? It has a lot to do with perspective.

I always ask students on the first day of class, "What's the first thing that comes to mind when you think of the word, *evangelism*?" Usually they respond with words like pushy, self-righteous and holier-than-thou. Then I ask, "What's the first thing that comes to mind when you think of the person who influenced you most for God?" They usually respond with words like loving, caring and accepting. I then reply, "When it comes to evangelism in this course, let's go for the second category, not the first."

Before we can begin to do evangelism, we sometimes need to overcome areas of resistance to the task itself. Believe it or not, these can be fairly easily obviated once we understand just what is at stake and the principles involved.

People are most often resistant to evangelism for at least three reasons—they lack motivation; they fear rejection; they assume inadequacy. Let's look at these one at a time.

**We Lack Motivation**

Some years ago I was sitting in a sauna with a young man I did not know. As we were getting acquainted, I soon found that he was a Muslim from Indonesia. At one point I asked him if he had ever considered Christianity. He replied: "No, why should I?" I then asked: "What do you do for a living?" He was an engineer. After thinking for a moment I asked again, "What do you do when you have a fifty-ton block of concrete? How do you move it?" He smiled a bit and said, "You've got to have a hoist." My immediate response was, "Let me tell you about the hoist." Quickly I explained about the power of the Holy Spirit available through faith in Jesus Christ. As I left the sauna I motioned with my hand pretending to raise an imaginary block and reminded him, "Remember the hoist." Somewhat to my surprise he smiled again and promised not to forget. The next day I caught sight of him across a crowded room. When he saw me he motioned by raising his hand, pretending to lift an imaginary block.

I believe that every religion the world over (including my own) is a fifty-ton block of concrete without the power of the Holy Spirit available through faith in Jesus Christ. That illustrates the difference between religion (a fifty-ton block of "do's and don'ts") and a personal relationship with God through faith in Jesus Christ (the power of the gospel).

The intent of this chapter is not to provide a specific program for sharing the gospel. We've already stated that if we are not properly motivated, even a good program probably will never work. On the other hand, if we are truly motivated, then no matter what the program, we can probably find a way to make it happen. That is not to say that specific programs are not important, certainly they are. It is just that programs, to be effective, need to be designed with particular churches in mind—their demographics, their constituencies, their cultures and most importantly, the attitudes of their members toward sharing their faith with those around them.

We lack motivation because we do not understand the absolute necessity for the gospel of Jesus Christ. So what is at stake? Need I remind you that you do not have to die to go to hell? Too many are languishing there already—living in a hell of disobedience and lacking the power to overcome. Faith in Jesus Christ accesses that power. Here is how it works, once again from a little different perspective.

Briefly stated, the story begins with creation—actually before. Several passages of Scripture state that the Lamb was slain before the foundation of the world (I Peter 1:17-21). That means that God redeemed you before God created you. God loved you before God made you. Why would God create knowing that what was being created would cost the price of an only son? Because God's nature is to love, and love needs an object, the void was not enough. Furthermore, the nature of God's love is to be freely given, expecting nothing in return. It cannot be forced. Once again, if we cannot say no, our yes is meaningless. God also knew that the freedom to say no makes disobedience almost inevitable. In fact, with the exception of Jesus Christ, all have sinned and fall short of the glory of God (Rom. 3:23).

Some means of reconciliation was needed. The covenant with Abraham was cut for that purpose. There was even provision for covenant renewal—the sacrifice. Within generations of Abraham, however, the sacrifices no longer read the heart. God became weary of their mindless sacrifices (Ps. 40:6). That makes the new covenant vitally important. All of salvation history turns on these words found in the longest book in the Bible, "The time is coming," declares the LORD, when I will make a new covenant with the house of Israel and with the house of Judah.... For I will forgive their wickedness and will remember their sins no more" (Jer. 31:31–34b). The old covenant, meaning old testament, was not sufficient to root sin out (expiate), only to cover sin over (propitiate). The new covenant, however, empowers us to overcome those things that would attempt to consume us. In Jesus Christ we have a sacrifice, once and for all (Heb. 9:26). The result? We exchange the law of sin and death—our inability to measure up—for the law of the Spirit of life—the ability to overcome (Rom. 8:1-4).

Put all of this with the love of God shed abroad in our hearts by the Holy Spirit who is given to us (Rom. 5:5), and something else comes into play. One of the things that God does for us when we accept God's love and forgiveness and fills us with the Holy Spirit is that God enables us to see people as God sees them. I have always believed that God sees me as I see my own children. The most natural thing in the world is to love that which is a part of us. Since that experience in the closet described in Chapter 5, when I see people as I see my own children, evangelism takes on a whole new meaning. I think of Rahab in the book of Joshua. The instructions the spies she protected gave her were to gather her family into the house. They would be spared when the walls of Jericho were destroyed and the city was put to the sword. I would imagine that she did everything in her power to make certain that all her family members were gathered. I once told my son that I would do anything in my power to make certain he was gathered into the body of Christ. I will never forget the phone call late one night saying, "Well, Dad, you can begin to relax. I have just had an encounter with the living God." Need I remind you that we do not love people in order to evangelize them? That smacks of manipulation. We evangelize people because we love them.

I've described my conversion experience while still an undergraduate student at Duke University. At that time it was a rude awakening to realize that I was twenty-one years old and had never been used of God in affecting any kind of positive change in anyone else's life. From that moment I wanted to spend the rest of my life helping people feel better about God, themselves and those around them. I wanted to do evangelism. I was motivated, but I was an introvert. I had this horrible fear of rejection. Then I had an experience early in my ministry that would help to deliver me from that fear.

**We Fear Rejection**

I was visiting a prison (actually the county jail on this occasion) and was fortunate enough to see a man give his life to Jesus Christ. The next day I went to visit him (no doubt to polish him up a bit), and he met me at the bars. I shall never forget the first words out of his mouth. "Tuttle, I laid awake all last night thinking, and suddenly it occurred to me that it takes an average of twenty-five different witnesses before any real encounter with God takes place. Just because you were number twenty-five you think you did it all and you stink." Suddenly I had an incredible lump in my throat. He had me! Just because I was number twenty-five, I thought I had done it all when twenty-four encounters just as important had gone before me. Do we believe that? I would hope to God we would live like it. When we—especially we evangelical types—do not see the change take place before our very eyes we tend to go home saying, "I blew it!" Once I realized that inherent to ministry in general—and to evangelism in particular—there is twenty-four times more rejection than affirmation, I stopped taking the rejection so personally. The twenty-four no's are just as important as the one yes. Even the rejections themselves became a vital part of the journey. But wait, there's more.

It is always important to remember that God takes the initiative in the drama of rescue. We are not in this alone. God has more invested in our attempts to be faithful to the task of evangelism than we do.

Some years ago I was driving on a remote road on the North Korean border of China. We had seen no one for hours, and although my companion spoke Korean—a language spoken in that part of China—the road signs (when we could find them) were in Mandarin Chinese. I feared we were lost. Seeing smoke curling over a rise just off road, we pulled over hoping to find a house and directions. Our hopes were confirmed. As we knocked on the door, a woman appeared who assured us that we were on the right road but then invited us in for hospitality. How could we refuse? As she served us dog soup—it's actually not bad—I thought to share with her something of our ministry of evangelism. After some minutes I finally spoke the name of Jesus and immediately her head came up and she spoke words that caused my interpreter to blanch. I had to know, "What did she say?" He said, "She said, 'So that's his name.'"[1]

I mentioned in an earlier chapter some outlines that I had written for talks in an experience called The Emmaus Walk. One of the outlines was entitled "Prevenient Grace." Prevenient grace describes the work of the Holy Spirit in the life of the pre-Christian between conception and conversion. During that time the Spirit of God woos us or prevents us from moving so far from the way that we finally understand the claims of the gospel upon our lives. The Holy Spirit guarantees our freedom to say yes. Now if your approach is more Reformed (or Calvinistic), don't panic. This still works. Karl Barth insisted that it is Jesus Christ who was the "Elect Man,'" and we become the elect as we place our faith and trust in him and are baptized by the Holy Spirit into his body.

The point of all this is that the Holy Spirit is at work in your sphere of influence even as you read these words preparing people for your ministry. Each of us has a sphere of influence where only we can minister most effectively. As hard as I try, I'll turn some of your friends flat off. No matter. You have a sphere. I have a sphere. Furthermore, whatever gifts are necessary to enable us to minister effectively in those spheres are available if we are open and willing to obey God's call.

How many of you accepted the truth of the gospel the first time you understood its claims upon your life? God is at work from the moment of conception. In my book on the history of evangelism, I found that many of the most gifted evangelists were women—mothers and grandmothers praying behind the scenes. Note the reference to Eunice and Lois in what could have been Paul's last letter to Timothy (2 Tim. 1:5). The fact that some of these women might not be as well known as most of the men proves that much of what goes on in evangelism happens among the distant saints. These are the people who hover in shadows, pray for wayward sons and daughters, intercede for the people and persist before the throne of grace. God takes notice and responds—lest the God of justice and mercy be worn out by these daughters of justice and mercy. All of this, of course, makes reference once again to prevenient grace—this time to those early influences upon us that make us open and receptive to the gospel of Jesus Christ. Let me tell you two brief stories to illustrate the point.

Many of you know about the persistence of Monica regarding the conversion of her son, Augustine of Hippo. Reared by Christian parents, Monica married an irreligious man with civic responsibilities but limited means and a violent temper. He was not converted until shortly before his death. Monica, as a young widow, is described by Augustine in his *Confessions* as concerned for her sons and daughter. She pursued them with prayers, tears and admonitions, while living a life of simple piety, and led them to Jesus.

Few lives demonstrate the importance of prevenient grace more effectively than the life of John Wesley. God was powerfully at work in Wesley's life long before either his "religious" (1725) or his "evangelical" (1738) conversion. Wesley's home environment, his early training, a "religious friend," the Holy Club and the Moravians were all only a few of the instruments of God's prevenient grace. For example, in his *Journal* for Tuesday,

March 7, 1738, Wesley writes, "A day much to be remembered. At the house of Mr. Weinantz, a Dutch merchant, I met Peter Bohler. . . . " Peter Bohler, you might remember, eventually led Wesley—virtually by the hand—to Aldersgate where his heart was "strangely warmed."

**Prevenient Grace**

Now let's do a bit of theology. For John Wesley the doctrine of prevenient grace served at least two purposes. First, it preserved the integrity of our own freedom in the human response. Second, it guaranteed the validity of an evangelistic appeal.

To put all of this just a bit differently, prevenient grace is that work of the Holy Spirit, supernaturally restoring all of us—by whatever means—to a measure of free will by reminding us, convicting us, warning us, promising us, inviting us, waiting for us. It is God's initiative guaranteeing the freedom of our own response. In an age when much of our teaching and preaching smacks once again of works-righteousness—associating salvation only with that which we do, and disregarding the crucial ingredient of by grace through faith—this is a vital corrective. Like Karl Barth to follow, John Wesley put God back on the throne of grace, back in the lead role in the drama of rescue. Surely, "we love God because God first loved us." Indeed, we are more "known that knowing."

Let's get closer to home. Where would you be without the influence of that special "saint"—perhaps a mother or father, a neighbor, a godly man or woman down the street, a church school teacher or pastor used of God as a means of grace for the moving of the power of the Holy Spirit in your life?

It is also important to realize that prevenient grace is at work even at this moment preparing people for our ministry. Once again, God truly has more invested in our ministry than we do! If prevenient grace is universal, then the Spirit of God is already taking the initiative in the salvation of all of those who will believe. Our task—privilege would be the better word—is simply to move into the mainstream of God's continuing intercession, and to be faithful to those within our spheres of influence, knowing that God has called us to a ministry of reconciliation (2 Cor. 5:16-21).

I have always liked that passage in Acts 16:14 where Luke tells us "the Lord opened her [Lydia's] heart to respond to Paul's message." The prevenient grace of God was already at work in Lydia, a dealer in purple, preparing her heart to receive the gospel of truth. That reminds me of a line from the movie *The Color Purple*. "God is wooing us with the color purple and is really angry when we do not notice." God could win the world without us but has chosen not to. If God is going to do it in this age, God has chosen to do it through us or not at all. God has chosen to let us in on the fun of playing nursemaid to healing—body, mind and spirit. God, in effect, has delivered the whole world into the hands of the Church. That should make us bold. How long before we start to notice and "walk out the land"?

### We Assume Inadequacy

How many times have I heard someone say, "Evangelism is not for me? That is just not my gift. I leave that to those who are comfortable sharing their faith." We have already established that each of us has a sphere of influence where only we can minister most effectively. I still insist that historically those most effective in leading others to a saving knowledge of Jesus Christ were behind the scenes loving and praying, asking God to make them sensitive to those opportunities to speak a relevant word for God.

Please let me make an important point—*our greatest strengths are anointed weaknesses.* God does not use us in spite of our weaknesses, but through our weaknesses. I've seen God anoint pride and it becomes holy boldness. I suppose you want a text. Here is a great one:

> Now the body is not made up of one part but of many. If the foot should say, "Because I am not a hand, I do not belong to the body," it would not for that reason cease to be part of the body.... If the whole body were an eye, where would the sense of hearing be?... If they were all one part, where would the body be?
>
> The eye cannot say to the hand, "I don't need you!" And the head cannot say to the feet, "I don't need you!" On the contrary, those parts of the body that seem to be weaker are indispensable.... (1 Cor. 12:14-15, 17, 19, 21-22).

*Those parts of the body that seem to be weaker are indispensable!* In other words, some out there need to hear the good news from those who believe that they are NOT gifted for evangelism. Those folks out there cannot hear the gospel from those who do it well. Pay attention here! Douglass Hyde in his book *Dedication and Leadership* recounts his attempts as a leader in the Communist Party to train a man named Jim—the most unprepossessing man he had ever met. Hyde described Jim as grossly overweight, having a cast to one eye and being a most distressing stutter. He literally could not put two words together. Hyde, during an open rally in postwar London seeking recruits for the Communist Party, had stated that he could take anyone who truly wanted to be trained and turn him or her into a leader of people. Jim took him up on his challenge. Apart from the story of the transformation of Jim into a leader of people was the fact that it was, in part, his apparent disabilities that led to his successes. People would listen to Jim when they would listen to no one else because anyone with those disadvantages must be serious about the task. Furthermore, although Jim never really lost the weight or the stutter, people would listen more carefully not wanting to miss the point of someone who was that committed to his convictions.

Let me close with a word of personal testimony. I have already admitted that I am an introvert. My wife tells me that whenever I stand before the people I cut a vein. People, especially crowds of people, take it out of me. Also, since childhood I have had a stutter that has never completely left me. There are words that I simply cannot speak. Let me tell you what I've found. Over the years God has anointed those apparent disadvantages so that those former weaknesses are now my strengths. I find myself more reliant upon God. People understand it when I find it difficult to speak and then withdraw to a smaller cluster of people. It feels more manageable. They come to me and sympathize saying, in effect, if you can do it, we can do it.

**God Make Me Aware . . .**

Let's review. Overcoming barriers to the task of ministry for the next generation has to do with perspective. First, it means being properly motivated. When we understand just what is at stake—accessing the power of the Holy Spirit through personal faith in Jesus Christ so that we can overcome the things that would attempt to consume us—we find it so much easier to speak the timely word or do the timely deed. In addition, motivation takes on an added urgency once we realize just how much God has invested in our attempts to minister. God redeemed us before God created us. God, as a God of love, paid the price for our redemption, the forgiveness of our sins and the subsequent power we need to overcome. God then gives us the fruit of the Spirit so that we can see people as God sees them, as we see our own children. God gifts us with whatever gifts that are necessary to enable us to minister effectively. Know it, believe it, expect it and act upon it.

The fear of rejection is also an issue of perspective. Inherent to ministry in general and evangelism in the specific—"specific" being a word I can never pronounce—is twenty-four times more rejection than affirmation. Once we realize that fact we do not take it so personally, acknowledging that the twenty-four no's are just as important as the one yes. Additionally, God then takes the initiative in the drama of rescue. Even as you read these words, the Holy Spirit is at work in your sphere of influence preparing people for your ministry. We are not in this alone.

Finally, we too easily assume inadequacy because we do not realize that our greatest strengths are anointed weaknesses. God does not use us in spite of our weaknesses, but through our weaknesses. Someone out there needs to receive from you because of who you are—the good, the bad, even the indifferent.

All of this is to say, *we can do this*. God can use our lives in effecting positive eternal change in the hearts and lives of others. That promises meaning and purpose beyond ourselves, and that is what life is all about. As you anticipate your future let me leave you with this challenge. Pray this prayer as you address each new day, "God, make me aware of my opportunities for ministry, where you are already at work, and then give me the courage to speak the word and do the deed with boldness and love. Amen."

## End Notes

[1] Don Richardson's, *Eternity in Their Hearts*, tells a similar story.

# CONCLUSION
## (THE CHALLENGE)

I like sunrises. This photo is taken at sunrise from a small plane just skimming the Alps between Zagreb and Munich. All good conclusions should be full of sunrises.

Last year I was asked to speak to 300 high school students after a football game at a pizza party (10:30 at night). I got up and said, "I'm sixty-four years old. You know what that means?" They all shouted in unison, "You're old." I said, "You're right, but it also means that twenty-five years from now I'm in the ground and you're still in your prime. Do you want me to stand up here and sing and dance and pretend to entertain you (which I cannot do), or do you want me to tell you something that will change your lives forever?" They actually shouted again, "Tell us something!" Thank God the gospel is interesting. I told them about Jesus. I told them that they were loved by

God, and together, if we had guts enough to watch each other's backs and then show up and pay attention, we would not only win football games, we could retake planet earth for God! They actually applauded. Now that's a sunrise!

The last chapter responded to the question about passing the faith on to the next generation; born again, what then? We addressed the issue of why it is so difficult to overcome our reluctance to share our faith with those around us. Honest doubt might still ask, "What's the point? Surely no one is going to hell because of my disobedience (where is the justice in that?)."

Furthermore, even if you are a fairly new Christian you might be asking, "What's the playing field like today? What are unchurched (or dechurched) peoples really like now? Have the rules of engagement changed since I was converted?"

Relax! Remember that God has more invested in your life and ministry than you do. God really does play the principle role in the drama of rescue. Being a Christian and then sharing your faith does not have to be the dreaded chore. In my experience, the privilege of talking and doing Jesus gives us meaning and purpose beyond ourselves as God uses us, the Church, as an instrument of grace for affecting positive, eternal change in the hearts and lives of others. Another sunrise.

### So, What Have We Learned?

What of honest doubt? Honest doubt raises the questions out of an inquiring mind, but never dismisses the case before listening to all of the evidence. Atheism assumes too much— that there is no God (in large part) because God allows things to happen and will not force the issue of faith and trust beyond our willingness to receive.

I believe that honest doubt is bred of an open mind, and that always gives the honest doubter the edge. If we are open to a word from on high, God has a fresh insight, perhaps some needed blessing, for each of us. As I sometimes stand in the pulpit, I thoroughly enjoy the opportunity of calling the people to worship. I usually remind them that God sits in every pew and tugs at every heart and has something specific for each of them in that moment. I then advise them to refuse to budge until God has given them what it is that God wants them to receive on that particular day. "If you leave this place without receiving what it is that God wants you to receive, you've been ripped off, and, quite frankly, we've been ripped off enough!" My prayer, as I write these words, is that God will bless you and that you will refuse to put this book down until more and more honest doubt has slipped into more and more enduring faith.

So, what of enduring faith? A song in a movie about the assassination of Bobby Kennedy, "You Never Gonna Break My Faith," states that God will sustain faith in the midst of trouble. We have learned that faith is a gift from God. If we are willing to commit all that we know of ourselves to all that we know of God (and are ready to listen), the Spirit of God bears witness with our spirits that we are children of God so that faith really is "being sure of what we hope for and certain of what we do not see" (Heb. 11:1). More sunrises.

### The Challenge

At the end of the chapter "Can God's Call on My Life Be Renewed?" I gave a challenge in response to the question, "Where Do I Go from Here?" Let me now reword that challenge as it relates to the book as a whole.

Let's see if I've got this straight. Right or wrong, Christianity claims that Jesus did something for us that no one else can do. Right?

If I repent and believe, then God will forgive my sins, no matter what I've done. Right?

Even if I'm holding deep-seated resentments toward someone else, if I'm willing for God to take them from me, that person will have less and less control over my life. Right?

Repentance and faith create low pressure so that the Holy

Spirit will come into my life and empower me to overcome the next temptation. Right?

Even though hundreds of millions of people believe that other religions are the right way for them, if I become a Christian they are not my enemy, even if they persecute me. In fact, I might win them by loving them and making them jealous. Right?

When bad things happen to good people, that gives good people an opportunity to show the rest of the world how faith sustains them through bad times as well as good. Right?

In fact, as a Christian I would grieve differently in the face of death because Christians believe that Jesus has gone to prepare a place for us where we can spend eternity in the presence of the One who loves us most. Right?

If I were to become a Christian it would be important for me to join a fellowship of other believers so that someone who knows my name could watch my back and pray for me in close fellowship with other Christians. Right?

Christians vote but they vote Jesus, not their money belts. Right?

For Christians, trust gets them beyond the need for clarity just as faith gets them beyond the need for sight. Right?

No matter how far I've run, God has a perfect will for the rest of my life. Right?

Jesus is the only way. Right?

And even if I don't have all that worked out theologically, if I'm willing to commit all that I know of myself to all that I know of God, the Holy Spirit will bear witness with my Spirit that I'm a child of God. Right?

Furthermore, once committed, the Spirit of God will assist me in passing that commitment on to the next generation. Right?

OK, so what do I have to lose?

*You lose your bad self and you gain peace and joy forever and ever and ever... the brightest sunrise of all!*

# APPENDIX
## (A Synopsis of the Other Major Religions of the World)[1]

Honest doubt is usually curious about the other religions of the world. While I do not claim particular expertise (except perhaps for some aspects of Islam), here is a brief review of the other high religions in the world today (roughly in the order in which they appeared).[2]

### The Earliest Religions

Before describing Hinduism, the first of the world's high religions, it is important to say something about animism and the related ancestral religions.

**Animism and Ancestral Religions:** Most of the ancient indigenous religions of the world can be lumped together under the heading of animism. Animism may go back as far as the earliest known communities in northeast Thailand—the Ban Chiang—which is thought to date from B.C. 3000.

*Significantly animism underpins nearly all of the adopted religions of every region and culture and continues to exert a strong influence on most religions today.* Some have estimated that nearly forty percent of the world's population is presently animistic. Although there is no common thread in all the various traditions, some basic themes do seem to emerge.

Animists in general believe that everything has a soul—*anima* in Latin—or a spirit. That could include animals, plants, rocks, mountains, rivers, stars, the sun and the moon. Every "anima," is thought to be powerful. Worship alone guarantees their favor. The smallest neglect arouses their wrath.

Animism is attractive because it infuses the sacred into real life—a lesson for every Christian. It offers people a way to cope with their everyday needs and problems through healing, success and even guidance for the future.

Usually the Creator God is thought to be too big and impersonal for animists. Again, they are more interested in spirits, sometimes called gods, that are more readily accessible. Since these gods are not personal, however, in animism there are no revelations, no word from on high.

The many ancestral religions also find their devotion in indigenous roots. The best known, the Japanese form of Shinto, is still prevalent today with temples dotting the Japanese landscape from one island to another.[3] Other forms of ancestral worship have abounded, to one degree or another, on every continent for thousands of years. Although there is no apparent link from one civilization to the next as to how one's devotion should be expressed, there is one common theme, as with animism—worship alone guarantees ancestral favor; the smallest neglect arouses their wrath.

**Hinduism**: If animism and ancestral religions have no common thread that transcends from one culture to another, then we need to look elsewhere for an extant world religion—

sometimes referred to as "high" religion—that predates the Judeo-Christian-Islamic traditions. There is only one, Hinduism, and that by less than 1,000 years. This is an honest attempt to present my own limited understanding of Hinduism from the point of view of one who is at least sympathetic with the religion and/or spirituality of many of my Hindu friends.

Although there is no fixed Hindu creed as such, there is a tradition that goes back to c. B.C. 3000, sometimes referred to as *Sanatana Dharma*, the eternal faith.[4] It is difficult to describe such a tradition briefly, as Hindus themselves have a difficult time reaching consensus. If we are to understand the global perspective, however, it is still important to make the attempt.

Primarily of Indian origin, the 700 million Hindus today live mainly in Bharat (India) and Nepal. Hinduism focuses on a system of Karma and Reincarnation. Karma, meaning "work" or "action," relates to one's actions in this life that then extend to influence one's position in the next—thus reincarnation. Although the most influential Hindu writings, the *Vedas*, were not written until much later (between B.C. 1500 and B.C. 400), most Hindus consider them timeless and eternal.[5] The earlier oral traditions seem to suggest that the basic character of Hinduism can best be described as disciplined action detached from desire or earthly affection. Although I've found Hindus who were monotheists and even atheists, most worship many gods; some Hindus claim that there are as many as 330 million gods from which to choose. I once saw a dying Hindu man hanging onto the hind leg of a cow in the streets of Calcutta. Supposedly 10,000 gods dwell in the hind leg of a cow. Nonetheless there are gods that are considered by many Hindus as most important; let's begin with a divine triad, *Trimurti*.

*Brahman* has been described as the origin, basis and cause of all existence. Though unknowable, this Pure Being (*sat*) is the creator god.

*Vishnu* and his female partner, *Lakshmi*, are avatars (meaning "descent").[6] *Vishnu* is said to come to earth to restore order when righteousness is lost.

*Shiva* is the god of contrasts who, as a phallus-shaped pillar denoting procreation, presides over good and evil. Some know him as the Destroyer who, when accompanied by his female partner *Kali,* is the original "Lord of the Dance" as they dance out the creation of the universe.

Beyond the *Trimurti* most Hindus reverence the much loved elephant-headed god, *Ganesh,* who, according to my Hindu friends—when the proper *agamas* or rules are in place—is best known as the god of good beginnings and the symbol for luck in one's daily life.[7]

Hindu teachers, or *gurus,* are characterized as spiritual guides who awaken disciples to a realization of their divine nature. This is no small point. I once rode on a plane with a well-known *guru* named *Satya Sai Baba.* I learned later from those who were greeting him with flowers that he is considered an incarnation of *Shiva.* I found him to be interesting but hardly divine.

For some Hindus, Hinduism is not strictly a religion. So say some who are quick to point out that religion can mean to *bind* while *Dharma* means to *hold.* I'm unclear on the nuances here but what Hindus *hold* becomes an inner law that should lead them from ignorance to Truth. The practice of *Dharma,* the code of life, leads to the paths for the pursuit of basic spirituality.[8]

Unlike animism, Hinduism claims a word from "on high." Relevant to this is that the Hindu scriptures can be broadly classified as *Shruti* (meaning "heard") and *Smriti* (meaning "remembered").[9] *Shruti* refers to something heard by the sages directly from the gods, while *smriti* refers to what was remembered and written down. *Shruti* is generally considered more authoritative than *smriti* because *shruti* is believed to have been obtained directly from the gods through the spiritual experiences of Vedic seers and is, therefore, not open to interpretation.

**Judaism**: Though pre-dated by the traditions mentioned above, it should be stated that the biblical account of God's revelation to Abraham was, at least by comparison, unprecedented and unique. Nevertheless, we have demonstrated that, before any possible dates for God's revelation to Abraham, there was already a religion in place that could in some respects explain the creation of the universe, and the presence of good and evil. If exhibited a noble spirit that moved people into a stream or paths of existence (*samsara*) that characterized holiness as a way of life. So why would God, the Lord of the Universe, want to be known by a wandering Chaldean named Abram in the caravan city of Haran? According to Genesis he came from no family of note. His father, Terah, worshiped the moon-god. His wife, Sarai, was barren and depressed. Still four millenniums later he is considered the father of more than three billion people—Jews, Christians, Muslims. It is a story that has to be told.

Although God obviously was made known outside the lineage of Abraham, God was bound by covenant to bless Abraham's seed, forever. *Make no mistake, God's faithfulness to that covenant, demonstrated here but ultimately confirmed in Jesus Christ, links past, present and future.*

Abraham looked for a wife for his son Isaac from among his father's kin. Immediately we see the influence of Abraham in the prayer of his chief servant, "O LORD, God of my master Abraham, allow me to find a wife for his son today."[10] Rebekah was an answer to prayer. Her father, Bethuel, and brother, Laban, immediately responded, "This is from the LORD; we can say nothing to you one way or the other. Here is Rebekah; take her and go, and let her become the wife of your master's son, as the LORD has directed."[11] Even their children were an answer to prayer. Isaac prayed to the LORD because Rebekah was barren and "the LORD answered his prayer, and his wife Rebekah became pregnant."[12] She gave birth to twins—Esau and Jacob.

Isaac had many of his father's weaknesses. Fearful, he would lie about Rebekah, like his father claiming that she was his sister, when forced to Gerar during another time of famine.

Isaac also had many of his father's strengths. He heard and obeyed God, and God blessed him for it. In Beersheba God spoke to the son, "I am the God of your father Abraham. Do not be afraid, for I am with you; I will bless you and will increase the number of your descendants for the sake of my servant Abraham."[13]

The results were immediate. Abimelech, king of the Philistines, was so impressed with Isaac's continuing success that he came to Beersheba to make a covenant of peace, "We saw clearly that the LORD was with you. . . ."[14]

The faithfulness of the next generation, however, is spotted at best. Jacob was devious and driven, in part by his mother, Rebekah. Esau was rugged and impetuous; he sold Jacob his birthright for a bowl of porridge and quickly married two Hittite women who brought sorrow to his mother and father. Rebekah, in her grief, favored Jacob. Then, when Isaac was old, Rachel had a plan, the deception.

Jacob, whose name signifies deceit, disguised himself as Esau in order to receive Isaac's blessing. When Esau discovered the ruse, he hated his brother and planned to kill him when his father was dead. Before that could happen Rebekah sent Jacob to his uncle, Laban, now living in Haran, to find a wife from among her own people.

En route Jacob had a dream while camped at Bethel, where his grandfather, Abraham, had built an altar to the I Am God when he first arrived in Canaan. He saw a stairway to heaven, ironically perhaps similar to those that mounted the sloping side of the ziggurat envisioned by the people of Babel. Angels were ascending and descending and then, once again, the Word of the Lord who stood above it, "I am the LORD the God of your father Abraham and the God of Isaac. . . . All the peoples on earth will be blessed through you and your offspring. I am with you and will watch over you wherever you go. . . ." [15]

With this promise clearly in mind, Jacob journeys on to Haran. Most of us know the story of Jacob and Laban. Laban first tricked Jacob into receiving the hand of an older daughter, Leah. Jacob then worked for the hand of Rachel, remaining 20 years before returning to Canaan. It is significant that on the return—anticipating an uncertain reunion with Esau—Jacob encounters a man who wrestles with him in the night. When the man seemingly allows Jacob to prevail, until Jacob's hip is displaced, Jacob refuses to let the man go until he blesses him. At that point Jacob's persistence is rewarded as he realizes that he has wrestled with God—difficult for some of us to interpret—who changes Jacob's name to Israel. Jacob means "he struggles with God (Gen. 32:23)." This same name "Israel," eventually adopted by all the descendants of Abraham, would characterize their relationship with God, no doubt to the present. The name would also memorialize the schemer Jacob, who would receive the blessing, not by his own wits, but by the appointment of a loving and caring God.

Give the man credit, when God spoke Jacob listened. Immediately he exhorts the people, "'Get rid of the foreign gods you have with you [Rachel had stolen her father's idols before leaving Haran], and purify yourselves and change your clothes.'"[16] A fresh start!

Within years Jacob's two wives and two servants had borne him twelve sons (tragically, Rachel died with the birth of Benjamin). Unfortunately most of these sons—the heads of the twelve tribes of Israel—would, for the most part, hear without hearing. The most notable exception was Joseph.

Joseph was destined for trouble from the beginning. Though his father loved him most, Joseph had a way of antagonizing others with his favored status, especially his brothers. You know the story. Space will not allow us to do it justice. Simply be reminded that Joseph is sold into Egypt, providentially. He rises quickly, but is falsely imprisoned. He is forgotten by his family and friends but is restored again through his ability to interpret dreams, a gift from the Most High God. Joseph wisely states that "God has revealed to Pharaoh what he is about to do" in saving the people from seven years of famine.[17]

Joseph was blessed and was a blessing to others. He blessed Pharaoh and the peoples of Egypt. He blessed those who sought food from the surrounding nations. He blessed his family and, once his identity had been revealed, moved them (seventy in all) to the land of Goshen where they prospered for over four hundred years. It was not until ". . . a new king, who did not know about Joseph, came to power" that they were oppressed.[18]

The impact of all this, now that the story has been summarized, can be seen in numerous threads.

Isaac, by no means perfect, was obedient to the God of his father, Abraham. The nature of that God, as seen by others like Abimelech and even Bethuel, was One who would bless those who worshiped the Most High God faithfully and exclusively.

Jacob, by no means perfect, was obedient to the God of his father, Isaac. The nature of that God, as seen by others like Laban, and even Esau, was One who would bless those who worshiped the Most High God faithfully and exclusively.

Joseph, by no means perfect, was obedient to the God of his father, Jacob. The nature of that God, as seen by others like Pharaoh and even his brothers, was One who would bless those who worshiped the Most High God faithfully and exclusively.

We obviously have a pattern here. God will bless all who obey by purifying themselves, by getting rid of their pagan gods and by worshiping the Most High God faithfully and exclusively. That is what Judaism is all about.

### A Time of Religious Ferment

It is interesting that although Hinduism has roots that predate the Judeo/Christian tradition, it found it necessary down through the ages to reinvent itself in the face of social changes and competition—especially from Jainism and Buddhism (see below). Most obvious, after the completion of the *Vedas* around B.C. 1500, *Brahman* became the dominant deity. Then after the *Upanishads* were completed in Sanskrit c. B.C. 200, *Vishnu* and *Shiva* become the dominant deities. The period under consideration was a time of significant adjustment for Hinduism. With the exception of holding on tenaciously to its rigid system of castes, Hinduism was open to change, especially with the rise of the more pantheistic Brahmins. In spite of this—or perhaps because of it—Hinduism, and then Buddhism, would spread along the trade routes over enormous areas of the Eastern world.

Since the many forms of animism and ancestral religions have no common thread, it is impossible to judge with any degree of accuracy any significant shifts in emphases among them.

Hold on to your hats, however; things are about to happen with a rush. *If you persevere here, you will begin to understand the challenge of the global competition and the contrasting claims of Jesus Christ in light of that competition.*

The sixth and fifth centuries B. C. were continually begetting new religions—at least five in all.[19] Since the dates of these religions are somewhat fluid (though all five surfaced roughly during the seventy years of the Exile when the Jews were in Babylon), it is impossible to establish a chronological order. So, we begin with the one that bears the closest resemblance to Judaism and Christianity.

**Zoroastrianism:** Persia was one of the many empires that would ebb and flow during the first millennium B.C. Zoroastrianism is commonly referred to as the ancient religion of Persia. Prior to this we know virtually nothing of the character of religion in Persia, although animism was prevalent in both Persia and Assyria at the time. Its founder, Zoroaster (c. B.C. 630-550), though born in Media, had a prophetic career that flourished under the protection of Persian kings.[20] One such benefactor was a king named Gushtasp, a name sometimes identified with that of Hystaspes, the father of Darius, the father of Xerxes, the husband of the biblical Esther. Though the identification of Gushtasp with Hystaspes, the father of Darius, is difficult to confirm, the dates are right and it pricks the imagination—a thought too delicious to dismiss—especially when we begin to identify the basic tenants.

It is thought that Zoroaster was originally a Magian priest or magi but soon reformed or purified the Median creeds that had much in common with an earlier Hinduism. His teachings are preserved in the *Avesta*. Most prevalent is a kind of monotheism that introduced the idea of individual salvation through the free choice of the god *Ahuramazda* (the Lord Wisdom) over *Ahriman* (the Spiritual Enemy). Incumbent to all this was an understanding of the powers of good and evil that far outstretched the understanding of Job's miserable comforters. This form of dualism pits the one god, *Ahuramazda,* who leads the forces of good against *Ahriman,* who heads the hosts of evil.

Judging from the so-called Zoroastrian motto, "Good thoughts, good words, good deeds" (the *Humata,* the *hūkhta,* and the *hvarshta),* it is clear that Zoroastrians place a great deal of emphasis upon the responsibility of choice—good or evil, positive or negative, even ritually pure or impure—in their quest of an afterlife.[21] Their dead bodies could not be buried or burned or thrown into water, but had to be left on high places for the birds to pick their bones dry.[22] Purity of body and soul were important. Perhaps because of an influence from their animistic relatives, scrupulous care was to be taken in keeping the elements of earth, fire and water free from defilement of any kind. Truth, whether in speaking or in honest trade, was the basis of every action. There was always the exhortation to be kind and generous. Agriculture and even cattle raising were prescribed as religious duties. Marriage within the community of the faithful was strongly encouraged.[23]

The theology, as such, obviously has some things in common with Judaism. Today, however, one or two superstitious practices seem to distract from the overall schema, such as the propitiation of the powers of evil suggesting the survival of demoniacal rites that Zoroaster actually condemned. Although some scholars are divided as to who influenced whom (though for my part the fact that the Hebrew tradition predates Zoroastrianism by some 2,000 years is significant), their proximity during this time is worthy of note.

**Jainism:** During this same time frame the lesser-known Jainism appeared in northern India.[24] It would serve as an intermediate system of belief between Hinduism (or Brahminism, the more commonly known name for Hinduism during this period) and Buddhism. It is significant that Hindus considered the Jains heretics, and the Jain antagonism toward Hinduism, specially its sacred system of castes, bore a striking resemblance to an emerging Buddhism.[25] Founded by an aspiring Brahmin ascetic named Mahavira (born c. B.C. 580), the son of a local raja who held sway over a small district in the neighborhood of Benares, the name Jainism is derived from *jina,* conqueror, a characteristic popularly attributed to the reputation of its founder. At age thirty Mahavira felt the emptiness of a life of pleasure and totally renounced his princely life to become an ardent follower of the Brahmin ascetics—a barefoot mendicant preaching his message of non-violence and renouncing the world. The latter included abandoning his wife, wealth and home and, for the next twelve years, spending his time in silence and deep meditation, often going totally without food and clothing. According to Jainist tradition, at the end of this period Mahavira achieved *keval-jnana* or "perfect perception, knowledge and bliss."

Even more significantly Mahavira, weary of the Hindu preoccupation with the myriads of gods, is, like Buddhism, basically non-theistic, preaching atheism or the absence of gods.

Although holding to a form of reincarnation, Jainism also believes that one can achieve salvation through freeing oneself from the wheel of birth and rebirth.[26] *Karma*, according to Jains, binds the soul to the physical world. Sins accumulate *karma*, whereas meditation and fasting burns *karma*. One can get salvation, freedom from rebirth, only by burning the *karma* that has accrued in the past.

By way of summary, Mahavira laid down five ways to get rid of the wheel of life: speak the truth; be celibate; own nothing; accept nothing that is not freely given; but above all, do not destroy life.[27] As the Zoroastrian speaks of the *Humata*, the *hūkhta*, and the *hvarshta*—good thoughts, good words, and good deeds, the Jainist speaks of the three jewels—right belief, right knowledge and right conduct. Right belief embraces faith in Mahavira as the true teacher of salvation and the acceptance of the Jainist scriptures as the authoritative teaching.[28] Right knowledge embraces the basic religious view of life in the search for truth. Right conduct embraces the ethical precepts inherent in renouncing the world.

**Buddhism**: Buddhism, like Jainism, began as a reform movement within Hinduism. Its founder, Siddharta Gautama (B.C. 563-483), like Mahavira before him, began a quest for truth by renouncing all princely comforts, embracing a period of asceticism and strongly repudiating the Hindu caste system. While Mahavira achieved perfect perception, knowledge, and bliss, Gautama, while meditating under a Bodhi (or Bo) tree, received enlightenment about "the middle path." From this point on he would be called the Buddha—the enlightened one.

As the Zoroastrian speaks of good thoughts, good words and good deeds, and the Jainist speaks of right belief, right knowledge and right conduct, the Buddhist speaks of the triple gem—the Buddha, the Law and the Order.

The Buddha rejected many of the Hindu concepts of ritual and worship. That alone invited resistance from the country that was obsessed with its understanding of how best to engage the spirits abroad. The Hindu preoccupation with pleasing images of impotent gods disillusioned him. His response: there are no gods to be appeased; there are no gods to be worshiped; there are no gods to distract us from the goal of true religion. He offered instead a search for the kind of truth that would give us the kind of fulfillment that would enable us to live peacefully one with another. Although the Buddha would reject notions of a transcendent God, his search for the path would engage peoples around the world on an inward journey that would at least offer them peace.

The Law, *dharma,* or teaching, has a belief in *karma* ("work or "action") that, as in Hinduism and Jainism, influences the flow and character of one's existence from one life to the next.[29] Buddhists, however, having no concept of soul, *anatta,* that would transmigrate from one body to the next (reincarnation), prefer the term "rebirth." One's *karma*—and this is no small point—simply gathers energy to give birth to a whole new being who represents the net *karma* of the earlier being.

The heart of the Law can be captured in *The Four Noble Truths.* Stated briefly, they are *dukkh,* all life entails suffering; *tanha,* the cause of suffering is worldly desire; *nirodha,* suffering ends when such desire has ceased and one is freed from the cycle of rebirth *(samsara),* attaining *nirvana;* and *marga,* the way to remove the desire is the Noble Eight-fold Path— right views, right motives, right speech, right conduct, right means of livelihood, right effort, right mindfulness and right contemplation—the essence of wisdom, ethical conduct and mental discipline.

The Order, *sang-ha,* (community of monks) provides the proper setting for all of this to take place. One cannot embrace the noble truths in the world—now pay attention, Christians— one cannot embrace the noble truths on one's own.

The varieties of Buddhism are many. A least twelve major sects have surfaced over the centuries, but for the sake of time and space, let me mention just two—the largest and the most popular in the West today.

*Theravada,* meaning "the doctrine of the elders," is the largest and perhaps closest to the original teachings. Quite simply it is non-theistic in theory, though I have seen old animistic and even polytheistic practices held side by side. Today, *Theravada* Buddhism is found in Thailand, Myanmar, Cambodia, Laos and Sri Lanka. Two years ago I was in Cambodia. I had the privilege of spending two hours with the monk responsible for the administration of the great temple across from the royal palace in Phnom Penh. After some time I asked him about Buddhist worship. He immediately reacted, "What is worship?" And I replied, "That which gives us an awareness of God's presence in our midst." His response: "You do not understand *Theravada* Buddhism. We have no concept of a transcendent God. Our religion is an inward journey." I should have known better.

*Zen* Buddhism, primarily associated with Japan because of the mother Temple in Kyoto, is the most popular Buddhist sect in the West today. *Zen* actually originated in China. As a truly unique form of Buddhism, it is sometimes said to be the world's most difficult religion to understand. It is no doubt influenced somewhat by Taoism (see below). It has no doctrine or creed, and is totally independent of concepts, techniques or rituals. Typical to *Zen* is the *Zen* master giving a devotee a riddle (*koan*) upon which to meditate. The classical *koan* is the sound of one hand clapping. As one's thinking is pushed to the limits of the absurd, one is said to arrive at enlightenment (*satori*).

Buddhism, still enormously popular in some parts of the East, was virtually swallowed up by Hinduism in the land of its birth. Few Buddhists now live in India. While Hinduism was continuing to refine itself, Buddhism moved elsewhere, but not without significant influence. That story takes us farther east across the Bay of Bengal and beyond.

**Taoism**: While Buddhism was making its way into China, two more philosophical religions were finding their feet as well—Taoism (pronounced Daoism) and Confucianism.

Taoism has been called the indigenous religion of China, although it would not begin to adopt its more religious characteristics until the second century A.D.[30] The life of its founder and greatest teacher, Lao-tzu, is shrouded in mystery and myth. Probably born sometime in the mid-sixth century B.C., Lao-tzu was a contemporary of Confucius (B.C. 551-479). Although we know that he was the keeper of the imperial library, he disappeared to the west in his old age, leaving behind only the *Tao Te Ching* (the *Book of Tao and Virtue*).[31] About 5,000 words long—somewhat shorter than this appendix—Taoism would nevertheless derive its name from this book, use it as a guide for the cultivation of the self and find in it a manual for political and social transformation. A second significant leader, Chuang-tzu, would further refine and popularize the earliest principles of Taoism some two hundred years later.

Taoists believe *Tao* (or Way) to be the cosmic, mysterious, and ultimate principle underlying form, substance, being and change. *Tao* encompasses everything. It can be used to understand the universe, nature and even the human body. For example, "*Tao* gives birth to the One, the One gives birth to the Two, the Two emerges as the Three and the Three give birth to all things. All things then carry the *Yin* and the *Yang*, deriving their vital harmony from the proper blending of the two vital forces."[32] *Tao* is the cause of change and the source of all nature, including humanity. Everything from quantum physics to solar systems consists of two primary elements of existence, *Yin* and *Yang* forces, which represent all opposites. These two forces are complementary elements in any system and result in the harmony or balance of the system. All systems coexist in an interdependent network. The dynamic tension between *Yin* and *Yang* forces in all systems results in an endless process of change: production and reproduction and the transformation of energy.

*Tao* and virtue are said to be the same coin with different sides. *Tao* creates and virtue sustains could summarize the entire system. The highest virtue, according to Lao-tzu, is achieved through non-action. Since virtue is the creation of *Tao*, virtue is natural to all people and should require little or no effort to maintain.

**Confucianism**: Although there are legitimate questions as to whether or not Confucianism can be considered a religion, there is, at least, an interesting philosophy that must be engaged if we are to fulfill our promise of being truly global in our perspective.[33]

Although one can easily contrast Taoism and Confucianism, they obviously have similar roots. The *Tao* is important to Confucianism although in Confucianism the *Tao* has a more ethical bent than in Taoism itself—"the Way in which an individual, a ruler or a state ought to go, the Way in which heaven has been made regulative for human conduct."[34]

Confucius did not intend to found a religion; he merely wished to interpret and revive the unnamed religion of the Zhou dynasty. Confucius did not put his teachings into writing. His disciples would record his conversations and sayings in the *Lun-Yu*—the *Analects* or *Conversations*—after his death. In fact, if not for the Confucian disciples, his philosophy would never have been known.

Although we have already discussed Taoism, it might be helpful to compare and contrast some of the fundamental facts in Confucianism and Taoism. It is important that we see these two coexisting practices side by side if we are to understand fully their influence in Asia and, to a lesser degree, throughout the world. In a very real sense, Confucianism and Taoism are like night and day—two basic philosophies whose differences lie in the attitude toward life, with the former more structured and socially-oriented and the latter more flexible and nature-oriented. No question, Confucianism is a secular religion that focuses on the conduct and practices of people in daily life. Responsibility to parents and ancestors, for example, is a central duty, and its virtues include benevolence, duty, manners, wisdom and faithfulness. Compare that with a Taoism that is based on the solidarity of nature and humans—the cycles of nature in which all things return to their starting points through passivity, peace and meditation. Although Confucianism and Taoism have distinctively different features, these philosophies complement each other, and many Chinese believe that honest seekers are not "balanced" if they do not have a measure of both.

The Confucian system is based on several principles, one building upon the other. In the beginning, there is nothing. The Great Ultimate (*Tao*) is the cause of change and generates, as in Taoism but further developed, the two primary forms: the Great *Yin* (the passive form) and its counterforce the Great *Yang* (a great energy). The dynamic tension between *Yin* and *Yang* forces results in an endless process of change, of production and reproduction and the transformation of energy. This is a natural order, an order in which we can see basic moral values. As in Taoism, human nature is inherently good. If a human being cooperates with the Great Ultimate and engages in rigorous self-discipline, that person will discover the real self (the nature of *Tao*) and enjoy the principle of change.

There are four principles of change: change is easy; change is a transforming process due to the dynamics between *Yin* and *Yang* (a cycle of expansion and contraction); change carries with it the notion of changelessness; and finally, the best change promotes the growth and development of the individual and the whole simultaneously—it strives for excellence throughout the network.

To summarize, there is an interconnected network of individual existence, and this pattern of interdependent relationships exists in all levels of systems, from individual, through family and state, to the world and universe. The whole is dependent upon the harmonious integration of its parts, or subsystems, while the parts require the nurture of the whole. The ultimate unit within this framework is the universe itself. Self is a here-and-now link in a chain of existence stretching both back to the past and into the future to be shaped by the way an individual performs his or her roles in daily life. One's humanity is achieved only with and through others. As far as it goes, Saint Paul could not have said it better.[35]

Confucianism completes the story of the proliferation of religions during the one hundred or so years encompassing the exile.

### After Christianity

It is important now to return to Islam. Since we have already discussed Islam at some length in other places, let me give you a brief capsule here.

**Islam:** Muhammad (c. 570-632) was born in Mecca (Saudi Arabia). Deeply and sincerely religious, Muhammad knew a great deal about Judaism, something of Christianity, and was influenced by them both. By 610, through reported revelations from visions with the angel Gabriel, he believed himself to be the "mouthpiece of God." The words received were then to be conveyed to the people. These messages, or revelations, were later collected in what Muslims call the Holy *Qur'an*. So, Islam, meaning submission to God, was founded. The followers, Muslims, meaning those who submit, believe that God, Allah, is one. Related to the Hebrew *El*, the greatest sin is to ascribe partners, *shirk*, to God.[36] Although some first believed that Islam was a Christian sect, or heresy, it soon became apparent that when *shirk* was applied to the Christian doctrine of the Trinity, Christianity became the fundamental enemy. Islam's understanding of Allah places great emphasis on God's transcendence, thus the section in the *Qur'an*, "The Transcendent God of Islam." The gulf between God and creation is too great to be bridged. Jesus, for example, was a prophet, but Muhammad emphatically denied that God could have a son. Since Christians believe that Jesus is God's Son incarnate, closing that gap, Muslims believe that Muhammad's words were a fresh revelation, in effect, superseding such beliefs.

According to the *Qur'an*, Allah sent 124,000 prophets including Adam, Noah, Abraham, Moses and Jesus. Muslims believe that Muhammad was the last of these prophets and served as their seal.

Islam's understanding of truth consists of two fundamental affirmations: "I bear witness that there is no God but God; I bear witness that Muhammad is the Apostle, Prophet, of God." The confession of these two affirmations (*Shahada*) is the first of the *Five Pillars of Islam*. The remaining four are: prayer five times a day (*Salat*), preceded by ritual washing and facing Mecca; alms to the poor (*Zakat*), especially during festivals and the Sabbath (sunset on Thursday to sunset on Friday); fasting (*Sawm*) in the month of Ramadan; and a pilgrimage to Mecca (*Hajj*) at least once in one's lifetime. In addition, an optional sixth can be added, the holy war or *jihad*, meaning "striving."

Since most non-Muslims do not understand the difference between the various Islamic factions, let me review some of the material from an earlier chapter. During the Umayyad Caliphate Dynasty (seventh/eighth centuries), the capital was moved from Baghdad to Damascus, where it remained for the next ninety years (661-750). During that time the *Sunnis* split, due to an argument over the succession to Muhammad, into *Sunnis* and *Shi'ites*. *Sunnis* still comprised the large majority and today are predominant in most Africa countries, India, Pakistan and Indonesia.[37] They are led by community consensus, *ijma'*, and accept the first four caliphs (or Umayyad Dynasty rulers) as the legitimate successors to Muhammad. The *Shi'ites*, or *Shi'a*, tend to look more to a specific spiritual leader or imam who is viewed as God's representative on earth. They consider Ali, Muhammad's son-in-law, to be the first imam. Unlike the *Sunnis*, the *Shi'ites* have an institutionalized clergy who exercise great authority; note the power of the Ayatollah Khomeini and the present leaders in Iran. Today the *Shi'ites* are predominant in Iran, Iraq, Bahrain and Azerbaijan. Then, when the Abbasid Dynasty replaced the Umayyad Dynasty and the capital was moved back to Baghdad, the *Shi'ites* split again, this time into Zaidis and Ismailis. Since the differences there are more political than religious, let me mention just one other group—the *Sufis*.

*Sufism*—*Sufi* means "mystic"—is a mystical movement that began during the same period (c. 750).[38] In contrast to the more fundamental branches of Islam where Allah is far removed, these Muslim ascetics sought direct personal contact with God. With the present day rise of Islamic fundamentalism, however, these mystics are becoming more and more difficult to identify.

**Sikhism:** In the north of India in the "land of the five rivers," (Punjab) Guru Nanak (1469-1539) founded Sikhism. *Sikh* means "disciple" or one who believes in God as the true guru whose word has come to humanity through ten historic figures. Sikhs also look to their community as guru. Although Sikhs acknowledge a harmony of Hindu and Muslim teachings, their sacred scriptures, *Guru Granth Saheb,* clearly distinguish them from both. They are strict monotheist, yet God is popularly known by three names—*Hari, Sat Guru,* and *Sat Nam.* True worship sings praises and meditates upon his names. Image worship, pilgrimage and asceticism are useless. The world is illusionary. *Karma* and transmigration are important. *Sikhism* stands for a casteless society and the brotherhood of humanity while respecting the dignity and equality of women. Ultimately, salvation is submission to the will of God, to have a love union with god. Largely an ethnic religion related to Punjab, now part of India and Pakistan, there are over fifteen million Sikhs worldwide.

**Scientology:** Perhaps the most recent "high" religion (or perhaps more nearly correctly "Metaphysical Phenomenon") is Scientology. Scientologists are an interesting group of people.

It's a straight line from the ancient eastern religions through Gnosticism (I could throw in the Gospel of Judas and the Da Vinci Code.), through Mary Baker Eddy (Christian Science) to Scientology.

Apparently in the early 1950s, L. Ron Hubbard, a science-fiction writer, decided to make some money by starting a new religion. He is known for saying, "If you want to get rich, start your own religion." In six weeks he came up with Dianetics, which later grew into Scientology, sometimes known as "the rich man's eastern religion."

The final frontier is not space, but the spirit. His Dianetics dealt with the body and mind; Scientology deals with the spirit (thetan) that has been distracted for billions of years (when you become a scientologist, you must pledge allegiance to Sea-Org for a billion years) by negative experiences (engrams). Since our conscious minds (the *analytic*) are slaves to our subconscious minds (the *reactive*, clouded by engrams), the object is to uncover this bad karma or engrams by a process of "auditing" to become "clear." Pre-clears are initiates who are moving up the ladder, levels one through nine, and it is not inexpensive (some claim it can cost as much as $350,000 by the time you achieve level nine). You must address each level one step at a time. To attempt to skip a level is to invite disaster, even death (some critics have identified this as a bit of a pyramid scheme).

Auditing is done in part by an electronic meter ("e-meter") used to measure variations in the preclear's galvanic skin resistance as a means of locating engrams.

According to Hubbard's *The Creation of Human Ability*, creation is not *ex nihilo* (out of nothing), but the process of a subjective mental emanation or "projection" of the thetans.[39] God would appear to be panentheistic (believing that all finite entities are within, but not identical to God). What scientologists refer to as "Supreme Being" is purposefully left undefined and is not particularly relevant to Scientology theory or practice. Thus, the entire physical universe is a

"Game," a product of thetan ingenuity (designed for escaping boredom), which apparently emanates from an original thetan consensus to "create" in prehistory. Hubbard's *Scientology: The Fundamentals of Thought* insists that the universe (akin to Gnostic and Christian Science views) is a deceptive and deadly spiritual trap. Ignorant thetans are bound by engrams and think they are only physical bodies. As a result they are weak, impotent creatures enslaved to a material creation that inhibits self-realization of their nature as immortal spirits. In essence, the material creation, as we know it, is not only an illusion but also a powerfully destructive barrier one must overcome to advance spiritually.

Salvation is to free our pitiful thetan from MEST (matter, energy, space and time). We progress through the levels of "Operating Thetan" ("OT"), increasingly achieving self-realization (an OT is one who is more and more aware of, and "operating" according to, his true thetan abilities).

The key: the entire religion spins on the existence of "Thetans" or immortal spirits. This is a term straight from science fiction (a great battle eighty million years ago between Zenu, the Emperor of the Galaxy, and the usurpers).

Whereas Islam will fight you (*jihad*) and Hindus and Buddhists will co-exist (peaceful withdrawal), Scientology is a mixed bag. Scientologists have no land (except perhaps for the Clearwater, Florida, Flag Service Organization which is the world headquarters for Scientology). Hubbard spent the last years of his life (he died in 1986) on ships. Scientologists will defend its ideology, however. Hubbard's third wife went to prison, and Hubbard himself barely escaped several convictions on the heavy-handedness of their defense.

Hubbard's successors, however, are known for going to court, rather than going for me.

So, what is the appeal? Powerlessness (more than power) corrupts (they got that right). People feel powerless. The web site asks the question, "What part of your life do you want to handle? Unhappiness, stress, anxiety, depression, trouble thinking clearly, personal well-being, marriage, children, helping others, integrity, honesty, right and wrong, education, learning, communication, job productivity, achieving goals, financial success, living in a dangerous environment, drug and alcohol problems, personalities, emotions, how to deal with others."

Let me close this discussion with several questions for you to consider. Can you be a Christian and a Scientologist? Forty-seven percent of scientologists still consider themselves Christians. Before answering that question you would need to reconsider what scientologists believe about creation, about our own condition and about God.

**End Notes**

[1] Much of the information here is taken from my book, *The Story of Evangelism* (Abingdon Press, 2006).

[2] High religion refers to those with ideologies that demand allegiance and have transcultural significance.

[3] It should be mentioned that Shinto worship extends beyond the ancestor to include the Japanese family and culture.

[4] Since Hinduism has no founder, anyone who practices *Dharma* can be called a Hindu. A Hindu can question the authority of any scripture or even the existence of the Divine.

[5] The *Vedas* are called *shruti* and stem from the inner spiritual experiences of the ancient seers. There are four vedas—*Rig, Sama, Yajur and Atharva*. Each Veda consists of four sections— *Samhita* (containing the hymns), *Brahmana* (significance of the hymns), *Aranyakas* (interpretation of the hymns) and *Vedanta* (or *Upanishhads*—meaning "to sit down near" because the metaphysical dialogs are explained to students while seated near the feet of their teachers). It should also be mentioned that there are the *Vedas* or "Commanding Treatises," and there is Hindu literature called *Suhrit-Samhitas*, or "Friendly Treatises."

These Friendly Treatises embody all that is in the *Vedas*, but only in a simpler manner. These works attempt to explain great universal truths in the form of historical narratives, stories and dialogs. It is significant that these contain the *Bhagavad-Gita* (sometimes called the Hindu Bible or the Jewel of Hindu Literature because of its popularity) that describes a dialog between Lord *Krisha* and *Arjuna* on the battlefield before the Great War.

[6] Apart from *Vishnu* and *Lakshmi*, the most popular avatars are *Rama* and *Krishna*.

[7] *Agamas* are rules for the ritual, rites and the worship of gods. There are five of them adapted for the worship of *Ganesh, Shakti, Surya, Shiva* and *Vishnu*.

[8] One can argue that the *Vedas* show three clear paths: *Karma-kanda*, the path using the *vedangas*; *Upasana-kanda*, the path using the *Aagamas*; and *Jnana-kanda*, the path of the *Upanishads* (in realizing the *Brahman*).

The *vedangas* and *upavedas* are texts, which augment the *Vedas*. There are six *vedangas*: *Kalpa, Jyotisha, Siksa, Nirukti, Candas* and *Vyakarana*. While *Siksa* interprets the rituals and explains a path based on the other five, *Jyotisha* (astrology) is the most famous among them. There are five *upavedas*: *Artha, Dhanur, Sthapatya, Gandharva* and *Ayur-veda*. *Ayur-veda* (which deals with health and medicine) is probably the most popular.

[9] *Nyaya* (meaning "logic"), based on its origin not on the mode of its transmission, is a third category sometimes mentioned.

[10] Genesis 24:12, paraphrase.

[11] Genesis 24:50.

[12] Genesis 25:21.

[13] Genesis 26:24.

[14] Genesis 26:28.

[15] Genesis 28:13-15. In John 1:51 Jesus describes a similar scene where the heavens open and the angels of God are

ascending and descending upon the Son of Man. He himself is the bridge between heaven and earth.

[16] Genesis 35:2.

[17] Genesis 41:25.

[18] Exodus 1:8. The Israelites remained in Egypt for 430 years.

[19] Mircea Eliade uses the phrase "Axial Age" to describe this period of religious effervescence. Only Christianity (A.D. first century), Islam (A.D. seventh century), and Sikhism (A.D. sixteenth century) remain (although Scientology is included as a twentieth century "Metaphysical Phenomenon"). Since Communism has characteristics of a high religion—ideologies that demand allegiance and have transcultural significance—some believe that this should be included as well.

[20] His name in its ancient form in the *Avesta* is *Zarathustra*, and in later Persian, *Zardusht*, a form of Zoroaster, which is now common but adopted from the Greek and Latin Zoroastres. There are alternative dates for the beginning of Zoroaster's influence (B.C. 1460, B.C. 1350, B.C. 1200) but none so well documented as the dates included here.

[21] Zoroastrian mythology projected divine rewards into the afterlife. There was no escape from divine retribution, evil for evil, good for good. On the fourth day after death, the souls of the righteous entered the realm of the blessed, a place of beauty and endless joy. The wicked went to a place of woe and suffering. After a final rite of purification, the formerly wicked joined the souls of the righteous to share in a reconstituted world of the pure where there was salvation for all.

[22] Since Ezekiel was exiled about this same time (B. C. 597), it makes one think of the valley of dry bones in Ezekiel 37.

[23] *Vendid_d*, iv. 47.

[24] The inexactness of present day Jainism can be seen in the various estimates of its followers, from 500,000 to more than four million, mostly in northern India.

[25] Though it emerged in a predominantly Hindu culture,

Jainism rejects the idea that the Vedas are divinely inspired. The Jain resemblance to Buddhism can be seen in a system of monasticism that includes ethical teachings, sacred texts and the story of its founder. Although many scholars believe that Jainism developed independently of Buddhism and is the more ancient of the two, some would see Jainism as a somewhat later offshoot of Buddhism.

[26] There are four states of existence (*gatis*) into which souls can be reincarnated (determined by accumulated karmic merits or demerits): heavenly beings; human beings; *tiryancha* beings (animals, plants, and lower life forms); and infernal beings (those tormented in hell).

[27] A Jainist ascetic will allow himself to be bitten by gnats and mosquitoes rather than risk their destruction by brushing them away. Hospitals for animals have been a prominent feature of Jainist benevolence—bordering at times on the absurd. In 1834, for example, a temple hospital existed in Kutch that supported 5,000 rats. This gives new meaning to Annie Dillard's *Pilgrim from Tinker Creek*.

[28] These scriptures are less extensive and less varied than the Buddhist, and, while resembling the latter to a large degree, they lay great stress on bodily mortification. The canon of the White-robed Sect consists of forty-five *Agamas*, or sacred texts, in the *Prakrit* tongue. Jacobi, who has translated some of these texts in his *Sacred Books of the East*, is of the opinion that they cannot be older than B.C. 300.

[29] It is important to note that the Jainist view of *karma*—and its association with sin— affects one only negatively, never positively.

[30] Religious Taoism in the second century A.D. was an amalgam primarily of myth and liturgy, including spiritism and magical practices.

[31] The title *Tao Te Ching* means the canon of *Tao and Virtue*.

[32] *Tao Te Ching*, Ch. 42.

[33] Confucianism, like Taoism, would develop more religious characteristics during the Second Century A.D.

[34] D. Howard Smith, "Tao," in *Dictionary of Comparative Religion,* p. 601.

[35] Cf. I Corinthians 12.

[36] Like the Hebrew Yahweh, Allah cannot be pluralized.

[37] It is interesting to note that Osama Bin Laden and Al-Qaeda are Sunni whereas most Iraqis are Shi'te with a so-called Sunni insurgency.

[38] *Sufi* is from the word, *suf,* for "wool," what the early Muslim ascetics wore.

[39] Interesting parallels are here with the ancient Mesopotamian or Babylonian Creation Epic called *Enuma Elish.*

# Bibliography

Abraham, William, *The Logic of Evangelism*, Eerdmans, 1989.

Allen, Diogenes, *Christian Belief in a Postmodern World: The Full Wealth of Conviction*, Westminster/John Knox Press, 1989.

Chacour, Elias, *Blood Brothers*, Kingsway Publication, 1984.

Dodson, Ed, *Starting a Seeker Sensitive Service*, Zondervan, 1993.

Dyrness, William, *How Does America Hear the Gospel?*, Eerdmans, 1989.

Glaser, Ida, *The Bible and Other Faiths: Christian Responsibility in a World of Religions*, IVP, 2005.

Green, *Michael, Evangelism in the Early Church*, Eerdmans, 1970.

Hunter, George, *The Celtic Way of Evangelism*, Abingdon, 2000.

_____, *Church for the Unchurched*, Abingdon. 1996.

_____, *How to Reach Secular People*, Abingdon, 1992.

_____, *Christian, Evangelical, and . . . Democrat*, Abingdon, 2006

Hybels and Mittelberg, *Becoming a Contagious Christian*, Zondervan, 1994.

Hyde, Douglass, *Dedication and Leadership*, University of Notre Dame Press, 1966.

Johnson, Ronald W., *How Will They Hear If We Don't Listen?*, Broadman & Holman, 1994.

Jenkins, Philip, *The Next Christendom*, Oxford University Press, 2002.

Kraft, Charles H., *Communication Theory for Christian Witness*, Second Ed., 1991.

McGrath, Alister E., *Expanding Your Faith Without Losing Your Friends*, Zondervan, 1989.

Newbigin, Lesslie, *Foolishness to the Greeks: The Gospel and Western Culture*. Eerdmans, 1986.

Nida, Eugene A., *Message and Mission: The Communication of the Christian Faith*, revised ed., William Carey Library, 1990.

Packer, J. I., *Evangelism and the Sovereignty of God*, IVP, 1961.

Pannenberg, Wolfhart, *Christianity in a Secularized World*, Crossroad, 1989.

Richardson, Don, *Eternity in Their Hearts*, Regal Books, 1981.

Roxburgh, Alan J., *Reaching a New Generation*, IVP, 1993.

Smith, Donald K., *Creating Understanding: A Handbook for Christian Communication Across Cultural Landscapes*, Zondervan, 1992.

Smith, James, K. A., *Who's Afraid of Postmodernism?*, Baker Academic, 2006.

Stiles, J. Mack, *Speaking of Jesus: How to Tell Your Friends the Best News They Will Ever Hear*, IVP, 1995.

Stone, Bryan, *Evangelism after Christendom*, Brazos Press, 2006.

Strobel, Lee, *Inside the Mind of Unchurched Harry and Mary*, Zondervan, 1993.

Toulmin, Stephen, *Cosmopolis: The Hidden Agenda of Modernity*, New York: Free Press, 1989.

Tuttle, Robert G., Jr., *Someone Out There Needs Me*, Zondervan, 1982.

_____, *Sanctity without Starch*, Bristol House, 1992.

_____, *Can We Talk?*, Abingdon, 1999.

_____, *The Story of Evangelism*, Abingdon, 2006.

Uris, Leon, *The Haj*, Bantam Books, 1984.

Warren, Rick, *The Purpose-Driven Church*, Zondervan, 1995.

Wimber, John and Kevin Springer, *Power Evangelism*, Revised ed., Harper and Row, 1992.

www.ingramcontent.com/pod-product-compliance
Lightning Source LLC
Chambersburg PA
CBHW031347040426
42444CB00005B/215